Jesus In Your Skin

by
Scott C. Lovett

Fervent Fire Productions
Tulsa, Oklahoma

Unless otherwise indicated, all Old and New Testament Scripture quotations are taken from the *King James Version, 1769 edition* of the Bible.

Jesus In Your Skin

ISBN: 979-8-9888387-0-8

Copyright © 2023 by Scott C. Lovett

Fervent Fire Evangelistic Ministries
315 S. Sheridan Road
Tulsa, Oklahoma 74112

Published by Fervent Fire Productions

Contents

Origins 1

Nations: Ethos, Culture, and Religion 25

The Nation of the Name.................................... 45

Spread Among Nations.................................... 65

The Jesus Genealogy 93

The Jesus Race 117

Unlimited Descriptions 135

World Reconciliation 151

The Inner Man... 167

References.. 177

Change a Nation by Changing a Person

*The Lord gave the word: great [was] the company of
those that published [it].
Psalm 68:11*

This book is published by people like you, who want
to see people set free from deception and the tyranny of
manipulation, and changed for God's glory. If you
received a copy as a gift, someone thought it was
important enough to provide access for you by
purchasing it and passing that access on to you.
If you purchased this book for yourself, we thank you. If
this book touches you, instructs you, or opens your eyes
to truth, publish it for other people, so they can receive
the blessing as well. The message of True Liberty needs
to be published by the people who believe and receive it.
To publish this book abroad, go to **ferventfire.com** and
purchase discounted copies for your friends, family,
neighbors, church, co-workers, and even your enemies.
We offer both digital and audio copies. If you specifically
know people you want to bless, furnish their information
in the area provided and we will send them a copy of
their own by email. If you want to distribute the book as
a tool of evangelism for your church, simply ask for the
evangelism cards and enter your church information.

It is up to the saints to publish the Word of the Lord. It is up to you to declare His works among men. Pass this word along so that we can all return to the unity of the faith and knowledge of the Son of God - the fulness of the measure of the stature of Christ (Ephesians 4:13) and become, once more, one nation, under God.

Origins

In this generation of innovation, significant efforts have been made to reaffirm science's mental and technological achievements. The scientific community proudly stands with its chest out and its head back, with an ever-increasing skull full of knowledge that might make one believe that a new race of humanity has evolved to an era of supreme knowledge. Upon evaluation, I do not know whether all the present-day scientists would pass the skull size test developed by many of the predecessors of their kind. Can we conclude that this is a new species? Or is it, rather, the same kind that has always been, just taking ownership of the great human deficiency called pride? I would dare to believe the latter than the former.

While I do understand that humankind can attain knowledge, I am also aware that all of humankind possesses major flaws within its character. These flaws can blind us so completely that we are unaware of the ramifications of our humanistic ideas or discoveries. The idea of the superiority of man makes one's weaknesses even greater and the flawed theories even more harmful. Dealing with the origins of man has become a pervasive debate in our day. We state theories as facts as we focus on the outward, natural, created world and its basic biology. As we reduce the origin of man to an accidental combination of chemicals in a pool of sludge, we fail to deal with the true character flaw of evil and degeneracy that hopes for such an origin. We are so busy reducing humanity to meager natural causes that, when our sciences impart beliefs that cause men to adopt philosophies that evolve into evil acts against humanity, all the great scientific speeches and accolades become meaningless in the aftermath.

As science has advanced in its propagation of its theories on the origins of species, it has indoctrinated us into generations of racial divisions, class warfare, and a climate focused on ethnicity. Within each generation, there are those who propose the abilities of a certain race to achieve the ultimate goal of becoming the fittest group – some with so much success that they toppled the belief in the divine right of kings and the legitimacy of leadership based on the bloodline of royalty. The search for origins is often based in the desire of people to be the "first" race, or to be the one pure race, so they can rule above others. It is a desire to be a part of the latest expression of the unfolding of evolution. They believe only they will survive to continue the scientific responsibility of becoming the keepers of the earth.

These beliefs are dangerous because they serve to reaffirm that a lower species of humanity exists and must serve those with more evolved genes. It gives an excuse for those in power to execute decisions as a ruling class, disregarding the voices of the people below them in the name of science. The rulers know best, and the subclasses should gratefully take heed and submit. These ideologies provide the foundation for acting on what the scientists and government officials fail to see - their own deficiency and weakness to greed, power, and pride. This superiority complex deceives and blinds them into trusting perverted beliefs. They fail to recognize the existence and supremacy of God and thereby become the most egregious propagators of atrocity. They, as little gods, indoctrinate people to agree with their interpretation of life and oppose all others as ridiculous. Although they claim to support no religion, they become a religion, and propagandize their belief to the masses. Indeed, they are their own, greatest supporters, spellbound by the glamour of financial power and the thrill of global elitism. As propagators, they fail to see their errors. They are convinced they are superior in knowledge and intellectual prowess. Therefore, mankind must comply.

Such grandiose beliefs have been instituted between peoples, governments, and nations since fallen humanity began. The idea that a certain group of people is more just, a certain nationality, more righteous, or a specific race, born at a higher moral status is mere insanity. The primary issue is not concerned with the biological makeup of a man. The greatest deficiency within all mankind is centered in the inward character and beliefs which manifest outward, creative or destructive results. We are so busy trying to discover the nature of creation that we fail to look at what we are creating.

Man's ideas concerning these matters are always far-reaching. As nations of sin-ridden humans look for dominance in the world systems, they produce ideas developed by their God-forsaken thoughts and self-inflated egos. For centuries, ideas of superior and inferior races have justified the ill-treatment of others based solely on race or the conquered status of a nation. These evolved into beliefs concerning outward biology. One of the manifestations of these beliefs promoted the thought that skin color was creation's way of identifying those born to be slaves. As the ideologies of science superseded Scripture, even pulpits began resounding with the perverted, racist themes being spread by the superior man-made authorities in the land. Whole nations were

4

swayed and stood upon principles that are evil yet seem to make sense and offer the hope of good to people of the "right" sort. The question ignored or swept aside by men of power and greed is, "Good for who?"

In the present society, the ramifications of humanistic beliefs still exist. We have all been indoctrinated to look at people from the outside instead of from within. The lines and ideals of racial separation are being used in an intense way to bring further division and fear. The media and government officials speak in overreaching language that places whole groups of people into race-based classifications. Factions across our nation allow themselves to be manipulated into believing that a certain group is the cause, that a whole group is somehow more righteous or just, or that the sufferings of a previous generation at the hands of one race justify the immoral behavior of their offspring in the present generation. Many of the ideas we struggle with originated from past eras of science. No one wants to take those with "great" brains to account for the destructive effects their ideas had on society. Ideas move from the world's intellectuals into the social classes until they become beliefs that are practiced as social science. One of these "big brain," scientific theories of yesteryear is that there were races of subhuman creatures before

5

Adam which provided the genetic seed for the races which should be subservient to the Adamic races.

Today, we find ourselves dealing with the same concept under the guise of transhumanism. This theory was formerly known as polygenism and was thought of even before evolution tried to fill in the blanks in the fossil record by inventing stages and degrees of humans. Even while God corrected the sin of slavery within the boundaries of our nation through the Civil War, Darwin was developing a reincarnation of such thought with his theory of evolution. This was written as two essays, one in 1842 and the other in 1844. These essays would not be completely developed into book form, printed, and released until 1859. Initially, there were 1250 copies printed. As the civil war ended and reconstruction was initiated in the South, Darwin's book spread like wildfire and reasserted the scientific ideals of the significance of race, propping up the moral mandate for racial divisions, and reestablishing the power of various racially divisive thoughts. The title of Darwin's book was, "*On the Origin of Species by Means of Natural Selection or the Preservation of Favoured Races in the Struggle for Life.*" For those of you who might question what this title meant, Darwin clarifies his thoughts in a later book called "The Descent of Man," printed and published in

6

1871. These thoughts and so-called scientific discoveries provided men with a supposedly scientific reason to justify the ideas of racial supremacy, eugenics, and the "purifying" of the gene pool to produce the fittest race. As Darwin's popularity increased, his books were translated and spread among the nations, ultimately providing Hitler and other like-minded elites with the justification to purge their lands of the inferior races, and spread the influence of the supreme race, which was his reason for starting World War II.

As the study of eugenics and racial superiority infiltrated the minds of men, biological research exploited discoveries to justify the murder and abuse of humans. Corrupt scientists hijacked the biological research of skull and body sizes, facial features, skin tones, and all the other biological differences and used those findings to refine their practice of eugenics until they came up with five basic racial classifications which are still used today. These classifications are Caucasian, Black or of African descent, Asian, Indian, or Pacific Islander. Such classifications are not new. Early racial studies in the 1500s identified people in three groups Caucasoid, Negroid, and Mongoloid. This serves to point out that the nations of the earth have propagated superior and inferior race ideals even since the beginning of fallen man.

While governments, businesses, and those in development and scientific discovery continue to deal with people based on outward biology, class warfare, and manipulating the masses to advance their agenda of population control, acquisition of monetary and natural wealth, and pure, all-out global advancement, God views people from the ideas generated within them. He looks directly to the hearts of individuals and desires to work on people from within so that they will bring forth qualities and purposes that align with correct, moral principles. God is much smarter than we are. He only sees people's blood as being red and pumping through our veins. He goes beyond outward appearance and investigates the motive and belief of the heart. Out of this source comes righteous or unrighteous actions. While we live in a broken world and struggle to bring God's purposes into the natural realm, the agenda of man is the core issue that brings the meaning of outward actions to light. Man consists, first, of the internal spirit that animates the soul and leads to either bearing the image of God, bringing forth His divine nature, or the destruction of God's image, bringing forth the sinful nature.

8

As I write about these things, we must also recognize the abuses practiced by past theologians and religious organizations that reinforced beliefs that led men to further the advancement of atrocities. Mere outward participation and practice of religion fail to deal with the human heart. It is the relationship with God himself that calls man to account. The national church, government-run church, or church politics with any alternative agenda of racial popularity, mass appeal, power, appeasement, or gain falls right back into the previous agenda of the fallen nature. While religious practice deals with the external only, true experiences with the Word of God go much deeper to reveal the agenda of the heart and the character issues and flaws within man. Early on, much of the scientific theory of race found its affirmation within the walls of many religious institutions and doctrines. For example, so-called Biblical scholars identified the mark of Cain as skin color to try to make different races separate. This led people to identify whole racial groups as evil nations suffering God's punishment. While a multitude of people can come together and believe wrong things, be sure that God has his people existing in every civilization and people group. Therefore, trying to identify an entire population or people group as being the same is foolish.

The Word of God reveals what we see in creation and the study of various Hebrew and Greek texts also deal with the spiritual influence of good and evil, right, and wrong, and the struggle and deficiency of man himself. Though people keep trying to find a way to make everything a racial issue, we must realize that the sinful nature within man is the true issue. I dare say that, in God's eyes, examining us from within, we are identified by our inward heart motive more than any outward biological race. If we make the identifying factor one of the heart, to be a part of Cain's descendants is simply to do things your way, to be willing to harm your brother, remove yourself from God's presence and pursue money, cities, industry, and train your descendants to murder those in your way. If that is you, you are a descendant of Cain, no matter your racial origin.

To understand the origins of man and their differences, we need to start with the post-flood population. Recently, there have been several articles written by the scientific community that has connected human DNA to three male ancestors and three genetic groups. While so many take the Darwin approach, could it be that the study of DNA will lead true scientists, those who follow the evidence without preestablished bias, back to the Biblical account? To be led back to

Noah is not to be led back to just the population of the earth and its races, but back to the opposing natures warring within that population.

And GOD saw that the wickedness of man [was] great in the earth, and [that] every imagination of the thoughts of his heart [was] only evil continually. And it repented the LORD that he had made man on the earth, and it grieved him at his heart. And the LORD said, I will destroy man whom I have created from the face of the earth; both man, and beast, and the creeping thing, and the fowls of the air; for it repenteth me that I have made them. But Noah found grace in the eyes of the LORD. These [are] the generations of Noah: Noah was a just man [and] perfect in his generations, [and] Noah walked with God. And Noah begat three sons, Shem, Ham, and Japheth. The earth also was corrupt before God, and the earth was filled with violence. And God looked upon the earth, and, behold, it was corrupt; for all flesh had corrupted his way upon the earth.
Genesis 6:5-12

In this text, God does not start the flood account by naming all the cities, races, and skin colors. He opens our eyes to see that the sinful nature of man can become so powerful that evil thoughts become the primary thoughts of the populace. It also identifies that this is upsetting to God because that is not in line with God's intent for man. Apart from God and His ways, humanity has the potential to bringing the entire earth to the brink of destruction. In this passage, we see Noah as different than the others. We see words being used like "just," "perfect," and walked with God." Investigation into the Hebrew words connects us with his internal character. These words identify that he was righteous in his cause, sound, unimpaired, and having integrity, following what is true and factual. It is here also that we see the beginning of his three sons which would repopulate the earth. The Hebrew language is full of depth. Many scholars attempt to find the natural meanings of variance of skin color within the son's names, but then fail to mention the internal character of the three young men raised within the house of a man who honored the Lord.

These three sons watched as God instructed their Father to prepare for coming chaos and destruction. They probably spent years participating with Noah in the task of building an ark that brought them public reproach and shame. When the waters opened and the deluge occurred, Noah's three sons and their families were preserved in the ark of God for a period of one hundred ninety days. Once the waters receded and the families stepped out on dry land, God not only spoke to Noah, but to his sons as well, concerning the repopulation and the promises God would impart. After all these events, each son would make his personal choices and bring an increase in the character of fallen mankind or the character of God throughout the earth. Nations would be built, and customs would be established based on the inner character and beliefs of these three sons. In a day where people have been taught to focus on shades of skin, color is not as important as character. Within the same household, the character of each child will determine the results brought forth in each of their lives. Individuality can be so strong that it can be used to lead masses of people the wrong way or stimulate people to return to God.

Many times, the Bible uses the meaning of names to reveal the inward nature of the individuals that it addresses. The case of Noah's sons is no different and leads us to the motivations of diverse types of humanity in any populace. We will start with the youngest son by the name of Ham. The fact that he was the youngest represents not only age but the level of maturity and control. The name Ham has various meanings revealed to us in Hebrew. While its natural connotation is a person of dark skin tone, the character is the most important attribute. The character of Ham had the potential of strong protection when yielded to God, but in its context of being used in the fallen nature, it yields itself to the loosing of the passions. The emotions run too fast, anger goes too deep, and unbridled passions violate instead of protecting. Ham represents all the lustful desires of humankind, regardless of skin tone, because of a deep desire to achieve in all earthly areas. It is hooked to a growing lust for power and seeks to take land and control. In a later text, we see that Ham's passions are so great that He fails to respect his father and violates boundaries. As his seed spread throughout the earth, we see many nations and individuals in his lineage that seek to expand more and more at the violation of others.

Looking at Genesis Chapter 10, we see the development of each son's genealogies that lead to the establishment of nations. Like children can have distinctive character traits in a family, not all people in a nation have the character traits of a certain populace, but every populace is influenced by the condition and character of its national leaders. This is what people of our day would call "ethnicity."

And the sons of Ham; Cush, and Mizraim, and Phut, and Canaan. And the sons of Cush; Seba, and Havilah, and Sabtah, and Raamah, and Sabtecha: and the sons of Raamah; Sheba, and Dedan. And Cush begat Nimrod: he began to be a mighty one in the earth. He

*was a mighty hunter before the LORD: wherefore it is said, Even as Nimrod the mighty hunter before the LORD. And the beginning of his kingdom was Babel, and Erech, and Accad, and Calneh, in the land of Shinar. Out of that land went forth Asshur, and builded Nineveh, and the city Rehoboth, and Calah, And Resen between Nineveh and Calah: the same [is] a great city. And Mizraim begat Ludim, and Anamim, and Lehabim, and Naphtuhim, And Pathrusim, and Casluhim, (out of whom came Philistim,) and Caphtorim. And Canaan begat Sidon his firstborn, and Heth, And the Jebusite, and the Amorite, and the Girgasite, And the Hivite, and the Arkite, and the Sinite, And the Arvadite, and the Zemarite, and the Hamathite: and afterward were the families of the Canaanites spread abroad. And the border of the Canaanites was from Sidon, as thou comest to Gerar, unto Gaza; as thou goest, unto Sodom, and Gomorrah, and Admah, and Zeboim, even unto Lasha. These [are] the sons of Ham, after their families, after their tongues, in their countries, [and] in their nations.
Genesis 10:6-19*

Within each descendant of Ham, we find that a family is built that leads to a nation: out of Cush come the Ethiopians, Mizraim the Egyptians who operated the first mass slave systems; Phut, the nation of Libya; Canaan transformed whole societies, and his grandson, Nimrod, is known as a tyrant and people destroyer. He led masses of people to serve false gods. Through

Canaan, Ham's descendants fill the land and form all the Biblical "ite" nations (Amorites, Hittites, etc.). These nations merged into the empires that would conquer and possess the lands around them, from Assyria to Babylon, Babylon to Greece, Greece to Rome, and Rome to current day Palestine and Iraq. While these nations developed as independent people groups, the character flaws of Ham have existed in every nation, throughout history, that relentlessly pursued world domination and globalization at the expense of individual rights and freedoms. These people were filled with passion and lust that drove them to a condition with no moral restrictions.

While Ham was the youngest and represents a state of immaturity, we must realize that age does not guarantee the purity of character either. The eldest son's name was Japheth. His descendants would be the many Gentile nations around the world. The word "Gentile" comes from the Greek word, "ethos" which represents religion, customs, and habits that are taught to the members of a collective. The name "Japheth" is connected to people of light skin in the natural. But concerning character, it means, "to be open, open-minded, easily persuaded, naive to the point of being deceived, to be silly." In our day, the idea of being

16

open-minded is celebrated. To be open to the "ethos" of
the nations is praised as accommodating, tolerant and
fair. The problem comes when we begin to understand
that pagan religion and people's carnal customs do not
produce the character God desires. God's character will
only be produced in a heart that desires His nature. The
Bible reveals a natural progression in what science has
called "The Great Migration." Apart from God, the
nations of the earth seek humanism and substitutes for
God's ideals. The nations that came from Japheth's
descendants are as follows:

*The sons of Japheth; Gomer, and Magog, and Madai,
and Javan, and Tubal, and Meshech, and Tiras. And
the sons of Gomer; Ashkenaz, Riphath, and Togarmah.
And the sons of Javan; Elishah, and Tarshish, Kittim,
and Dodanim. By these were the isles of the Gentiles
divided into their lands; every one after his tongue,
after their families, in their nations.*
Genesis 10:2-5

The sons of Japheth produce descendants that
produce the following Gentile nations: out of Gomer
comes France, Spain, Wales, Germany, Armenia, and the
Miautso people of China; Magog is the peoples of
Romania and Ukraine, Celts, and the Goths; from Madai,
some of the people groups in Iran and India; from Javan,

some Greeks, Cilicia, Cypress, and the Britons who rose to power in the European Nations; from Tubal, the Republic of Georgia; out of Meshech, comes Moscow, Russia, and the populace surrounding that area; and from Tiras come Croatians, Bosnians, Albanians, and Slovenians. The Bible is so amazing in the fact that it reveals the natural development of nations. But the character of the people in a nation is what determines the leadership that is chosen and the state of a nation's existence. A nation's existence can be destroyed or overcome by the government and its leadership that adheres to wrong principles and beliefs. When people are taught an error, they become traumatized by those who were supposed to protect them from the very evil that came to harm them. Instead, they find themselves in a society that subjugates them through perversion and brokenness. We do not want to be a people that allow every sinful thought in our mind to take root. The greatest warfare people have is in their minds. Sin-filled minds produce imaginations that lead to non-remedies. These errors generate wrong beliefs that produce ineffective or deleterious methods to deal with a society's problems.

The third lineage comes from the middle son. His name is Shem. Shem represents a different type of people with a different character because Shem had a different desire. He did not get carried away with trying to prove to the world that he was open-minded. He did not allow his passions and desires to drive him to subjugate and defraud his brothers. Shem means, "medium-skinned" in the natural. But in character, it means "son of the name, good character, one who gives glory to God, one who is saved by the Name." No matter the fallen nature of man, God always retains a people that seek His attributes and His nature in the earth. Above the sinful, human existence, some people desire what is right. They seek to fulfill God's will on earth. When the earth seemed to be filled with people who were incessantly out to destroy one another, God had people who desired to show His character, likeness, and will to a hurting world. Here is the text that reveals the descendants of Shem and the nations they created.

Unto Shem also, the father of all the children of Eber, the brother of Japheth the elder, even to him were [children] born. The children of Shem; Elam, and Asshur, and Arphaxad, and Lud, and Aram. And the children of Aram; Uz, and Hul, and Gether, and Mash. And Arphaxad begat Salah; and Salah begat Eber. And

19

unto Eber were born two sons: the name of one [was] Peleg; for in his days was the earth divided; and his brother's name [was] Joktan. And Joktan begat Almodad, and Sheleph, and Hazarmaveth, and Jerah, And Hadoram, and Uzal, and Diklah, And Obal, and Abimael, and Sheba, And Ophir, and Havilah, and Jobab: all these [were] the sons of Joktan. And their dwelling was from Mesha, as thou goest unto Sephar a mount of the east. These [are] the sons of Shem, after their families, after their tongues, in their lands, after their nations.
Genesis 10:21-31

The descendants of Shem produce the following nations: Elam produces Persis which joins with the Medes and becomes Iran; Asshur's descendants merge with the Canaanites and become the Assyrians; Arphaxed produces the Chaldeans that merge with Babylon; Abram leaves Chaldea and seeks to follow the one true God; God's Spirit separates him from the nations and he builds a people known as Hebrews; out of Lud comes Syria; and out of Aram comes Turkey.

These [are] the families of the sons of Noah, after their generations, in their nations: and by these were the nations divided in the earth after the flood.
Genesis 10:32

As God dispersed the nations and raised the descendants of Noah's three sons, He went deeper than nationality or skin to determine those whom He would call His people. He is a God that seeks a people, and He dwells with those who seek a relationship with Him. Though humanity seeks to find validation by tracing genealogy and heritage, every individual must validate their relationship with God. Noah was not accountable for the character deficiencies or efficiencies that would penetrate the generations of his descendants. All mankind is born with deficiency and character flaws, but those who spend their time walking with God are taught to overcome and to manifest the image of God in the earth. While scientists discover the outward and natural existence of man, God alone has the power to amend an individual's inward thoughts, motives, and condition of heart.

God that made the world and all things therein, seeing that he is Lord of heaven and earth, dwelleth not in temples made with hands; Neither is worshipped with men's hands, as though he needed any thing, seeing he giveth to all life, and breath, and all things; And hath made of one blood all nations of men for to dwell on all the face of the earth, and hath determined the times before appointed, and the bounds of their habitation; That they should seek the Lord, if haply

they might feel after him, and find him, though he be not far from every one of us: For in him we live, and move, and have our being; as certain also of your own poets have said, For we are also his offspring.
Acts 17:24-28

God is seeking people from every nation who long to walk with Him. He is a God that is not limited to one nation, a single tribe, or an individual tongue. He is not limited by location. Those who seek Him will find Him and He will lead them in His ways of righteousness.

Being human starts with an internal sense of morality. This conscience is the awareness of a spirit that is made in God's image and makes us His offspring. Not all of humanity seeks to grow or nurture God's image by walking in a relationship with God. Without God, the nature of fallen man drives us to leave God's presence and shuts off the conscience so we can walk in the ways of the world. Though God seeks a people, the systems of the world seek a people too. They want a people that yield to the fallen nature so that the world order can bring people into subjection to ungodly men who desire to play god by ruling over others thereby gaining money, pleasures, perversions, and power. These men use government and law to validate the deficient nature thereby justifying the actions of weak and corrupt people. This weakness within man is caused by the sin nature and leads people to operate in a bondage equivalent to slavery. Yet, this slavery is not a bondage from without. It is generated from a vulnerability to sin from within.

People believe that God has excluded whole nations from His plan by causing them to be born into nations void of His Truth. There is not one human born that exists without a source of ungodly influence. But there are those who, in spite of that influence, choose to seek the Lord. God uses these to bring His ways and purposes to each nation.

Remember the days of old, consider the years of many generations: ask thy father, and he will shew thee; thy elders and they will tell thee. When the highest divided to the nations their inheritance, when he separated the sons of Adam, he set the bounds of the people according to the number of the children of Israel. For the LORD'S portion [is] his people; Jacob [is] the lot of his inheritance. He found him in a desert land, and in the waste howling wilderness; he led him about, he instructed him, he kept him as the apple of his eye. As an eagle stirreth up her nest, fluttereth over her young, spreadeth abroad her wings, taketh them, beareth them on her wings: [So] the LORD

alone did lead him, and [there was] no strange god with him.
Deuteronomy 32:7-12

No matter the sinful influence within a nation, God has appointed that anyone in any place can find transformation when they turn to Him. God can find his people in the middle of a desert, or in a place that seems like a God-forsaken wilderness. When a nation is far from God, He raises individuals to declare His name, and He knows how many of His servants it will take to transform His people and bring them to Himself. Often, we think that God can only send his servants as missionaries from without. But God is so powerful, He transforms individuals from within and, by them, liberates nations. He calls to hearts and invites individuals to a new life by forsaking the strange gods of a corrupted people. When men respond to God's call, they depend on the God of all heaven to lead. It is being led by God that transforms a man and causes him to bear more of God's character and likeness. It is God alone who knows and deals with a person's heart.

Nations: Ethos, Culture, and Religion

To know a person skin deep is to reduce a person's existence to the limitations of biological stereotypes. Knowing someone in this manner takes no account of the inward workings, the beliefs, or the character of the person with whom we are interacting. The use of racial stereotypes by skin color or biological features was introduced by slave-holding nations as a method to propagandize the populace and use visual human identification to keep those in bondage in their so-called "place." The timeline of world history reveals countless nations which conquered by war and took captives as slaves for their national advancement. The word "race" did not become a prevalent metric in determining the predisposition of a person to be a slave until the Enlightenment and the advancement of liberal science. In the ancient world, people were identified with the group they belonged to or the nation they came from, not merely by trying to sum someone up simply by their outward look. Other methods were used such as language, class, education, as well as the prevailing culture, ethnicity, and religion practiced by the people around which they were raised.

It has only been since the 16th century that government and science have come together to try to use racial factors to identify people as having a preset character. As scientific research has advanced, it has been discovered that racial differences do not occur based solely upon a genetic variance within a person's biology. Scientists have discovered that it is impossible to make separate races by looking into biology alone. Emma Bryce from Live Science summarizes an extensive biological study on race by saying "The problem occurs when we conflate [a] social habit with scientific truth — because there is nothing in individuals' genomes that could be used to separate them along such clear racial lines." Genuine biological studies did not verify the various doctrines of racism. Humans with wrong character and nature did. In the name of scientific advancement, evolutionists promoted the superiority of specific races and built structures to undergird racism that would destroy millions of people throughout the world.

After all this scientific research, there is much more to mankind than biological makeup. Though man's blood is amalgamated with biological basics, God established the parameters for people to become nations. These nations naturally gravitated toward areas which best suited their biological traits. I guess this is what scientists would call adaptation. It is specifically God's variation at work in the individuality of nations within His creation. Though we see people through outward identification as unique in biological makeup, we must understand that beliefs, character, and heart motive is where the problems occur within the existence of humanity.

Ethos is the Greek word for the character, beliefs, practices, and morals taught to individuals born into a group. It is the root of the word ethnicity. It is believed that there are almost five thousand different ethnic groups, worldwide, that have unique beliefs and ways of existing. These groups exist within the nations of the earth and retain many beliefs that promote class warfare, nation-building, religious structure, and various cultural practices. Ethnicity is not only taught based on the beliefs of the culture into which we are born but, is also chosen individually. People around the world research their ancestry, culture, and religious beliefs in an effort to find a sense of identity. As people embrace the beliefs and practices associated with their choice of ethos, they try to identify themselves based on a certain culture. Accepting a culture also causes the individual to accept the wrong beliefs associated with it. It can be as simple as a belief about personal origin or as extreme as harming people of a different ethos within a society.

Since all of us are born into nations and groups of people, we find ourselves immediately being taught the beliefs and practices of our surroundings. We grow within a world that has preset ideologies based on past experiences and the convictions of our predecessors. These ideologies help shape our thoughts concerning people that exist around us. As children, we take them as accurate and factual. Yet humanity finds itself influenced by wrong beliefs and subsequently fails in its efforts to do what is right and just. Entire societies are indoctrinated with the teachings and propaganda of governmental ideologues who run the nation or locality of which we are a part. Inescapably, we are inculcated with the mindsets enforced by those who are in leadership, from the head of a nation to the head of a household. In our day, we would call this culture. Culture is defined as, "all the ways of life including arts, beliefs, and institutions of a population that are passed down from generation to generation, it includes codes of manners, dress, language, religion, rituals, art, beliefs, and more." This is the core training and the beliefs imparted from generation to generation. Man-made culture is one of humanism's most powerful tools when it

28

is embraced by the populace. It can be good if those in leadership are passing down principles and truths based on righteousness. It can be deadly and keep people from living in freedom if the motive of the leaders doing the teaching is self-serving, wicked, or full of vengeance. At the very root of the word culture, we find the word cult. The truth is that all of us are born into existences that heavily influence how we think, what we believe, and how we should respond. To say that national influence and agenda are somehow outside of a system of beliefs is to display our blindness to the very world into which we are born.

Our society promotes culture as the answer to self-identity. By returning to the culture of former nations and groups, people not only pick up the things that are right within it, but they also pick up the wrong that is associated with it as well. They immediately take hold of the hurts within the culture that led to racism, social class separations, and fallen humanity's responses to the discrepancies that are seen within its past. When we look backward and lay hold of the past, we often drag the atrocities of sin-ridden people into the present. Instead of allowing the past to teach us right and wrong, good and evil, and the lessons we should learn from it, we ignore our character and become emotionally motivated to seek revenge for our ancestors. To look at our ancestry is to recognize that humans carry traits that are good and evil. It is our job in the present to be taught by God through "His-story" and choose the actions we will take. This struggle is not limited to a certain group but is warring inside all of humanity. It is unidentifiable by our DNA or our genes because it exists within a deeper realm of influence. In this context, we must understand that nations do not just multiply themselves by increasing the populace. They multiply beliefs, structures, hurts, successes, and ideas that directly affect the people who are called to live within their borders.

> *And God blessed Noah and his sons, and said unto them, Be fruitful, and multiply, and replenish the earth.*
> *Genesis 9:1*

At all times, mankind is in the process of multiplying. All the nations of the earth instill beliefs and have multiplied the influence of these beliefs through those born within their lands. It is the nature of humanity to expand. Corrupt governments generate situations that cause the populace to focus on identifiable outward factors, creating factions. They use race, class, or some other identity to bring separation to create emotional disturbance so that the evil motives of those in positions of authority are never investigated. It is easy to focus on the popularity contest and all the outward applause and miss the evil lurking in the inward nature of men to multiply their own power and prestige. We blame the people but fail to recognize there is another realm at work. Man either multiplies the nature of God, or a demonic nature. Through time people groups either grow in righteousness or grow in evil based on the choices of those who make up the society, causing the multiplication of the nature that nation embraces. Demonic ideals increase as the selfish nature of man dominates and people are convinced they are right apart from God. People multiply the fruit of pride. They exchange the truth of God for a lie. They multiply lust for power and possessions, craving the accolades of man. They build for themselves to satisfy their greed. They disregard God and try to make Him into a fable. They make up stories that cause people to turn from God. Everywhere God reigns on the earth, there is a corrupt, world system seeking to overturn His ways and to rule over things that do not belong to them.

In Greek, the word for "nation" is, "ethnos." It means, "a multitude associated or living together, a people group, or a nation." The root word is, "etho," which represents the actions or customs associated with the nation. These actions and customs are a direct result of internal beliefs. Internal beliefs are influenced by an unseen realm. They either give honor to God and His purposes within creation, or they result in people's misuse and self-nature. Pride and lust influence a man to be his own god or make a god that is like himself. As the nature of humanity is divided, so are the nations of the earth. They either submit to the God of all creation, or they are destroyed by the pagan gods of the earth.

Howbeit every nation made gods of their own, and put [them] in the houses of the high places which the Samaritans had made, every nation in their cities wherein they dwelt. And the men of Babylon made Succothbenoth, and the men of Cuth made Nergal, and the men of Hamath made Ashima, And the Avites made Nibhaz and Tartak, and the Sepharvites burnt their children in fire to Adrammelech and Anammelech, the gods of Sepharvaim. So they honored these lords and made unto themselves of the lowest of them priests of the high places, which sacrificed for them in the houses of the high places. They feared the LORD, and served their own gods, after the manner of the nations whom they carried away from thence. Unto this day they do after the former manners: they fear not the LORD, neither do they after their statutes, or after their ordinances, or after the law and commandment which the LORD

32

commanded the children of Jacob, whom he named Israel; With whom the LORD had made a covenant, and charged them, saying, Ye shall not fear other gods, nor bow yourselves to them, nor serve them, nor sacrifice to them.
2 Kings 17:29-35

But Jeshurun waxed fat, and kicked: thou art waxen fat, thou art grown thick, thou art covered [with fatness]; then he forsook God [which] made him, and lightly esteemed the Rock of his salvation. They provoked him to jealousy with strange [gods], with abominations provoked they him to anger. They sacrificed unto devils, not to God; to gods whom they knew not, to new [gods that] came newly up, whom your fathers feared not. Of the Rock [that] begat thee thou art unmindful, and hast forgotten God that formed thee.
Deuteronomy 32:15-18

But I [say], that the things which the Gentiles sacrifice, they sacrifice to devils, and not to God: and I would not that ye should have fellowship with devils. Ye cannot drink the cup of the Lord, and the cup of devils: ye cannot be partakers of the Lord's table, and of the table of devils. Do we provoke the Lord to jealousy? are we stronger than he?
1 Corinthians 10:20-22

For all the gods of the nations [are] idols: but the LORD made the heavens.
Psalm 96:5

The wicked shall be turned into hell, [and] all the nations that forget God. For the needy shall not alway be forgotten: the expectation of the poor shall [not] perish for ever. Arise, O LORD; let not man prevail: let the heathen be judged in thy sight. Put them in fear, O LORD: [that] the nations may know themselves [to be but] men.
Psalm 9:17-20

While many people find differences between nations offensive, we need to remember that there are individuals in every nation who are seeking the purposes of God on earth. We also need to be aware that whole groups of people can be led to selfish beliefs and can commit great atrocities and do damage to others through trusting fallible human philosophies. History has revealed repeatedly that any person without God and His morality can do great harm to the people within their nation. It also shows that wicked and corrupt leaders are selfish and seek more power, more wealth, and more pleasure. Sinful citizenship is not excluded in their guilty pursuit of pleasure either. The sinful nature will always grab the silver before it thinks of the harm it is bringing to

34

another. As generations proceed, the thoughts and hearts of future citizens can become wicked and forsake God, even if the nation had great beginnings with God. In these moments of apostacy, God will raise men and women of righteousness to preach to the populace. Throughout the ages, God has always sent his messengers to appeal to nations that were on their way to destruction. In every nation, there will be people who break away from the unrighteous part of culture and seek after God.

To seek after God is to seek after the ways of righteousness. Righteousness simply means a method of life that is right and in line with what God intended. No matter where a person is born, they must choose the way they will take concerning their own life choices. As we choose, we find out whether what we have chosen is good or bad based on the consequences of our actions. It is no different in the history of nations. As the majority choose, a nation finds itself producing a land in line with God's intentions or a land that leads men to greater levels of darkness. God desires to lead people to His purposes, thereby producing the best results, despite a fallen world. When men stop seeking a relationship with God, future generations are born into cultures that have instituted the systems of broken men. These

35

systems impact those born and set them on a path to go even farther from God than those who went before them. History also shows that, in any society that forsakes God, some people come awake internally and realize the destitute condition within themselves, their family, and their society. Instead of being led externally through outward controls, God leads these individuals from their hearts. This is what happened in the days of Abram.

Nine generations of men had been born since the days of Noah, and the majority had followed their fallen nature. Abram was born into a family that found its life intertwined with the developing systems of a sin-filled world. The men of the earth sought power, government, national dominance, and people who would yield to fulfill their wicked desires. As Abram aged, he became internally aware of the external conditions. It was here he chose to leave his culture and ethos and follow the one true God. He was not born into a God-fearing society, or a Jewish culture, because he would be the first to take the steps to restore Godly existence. He would hear the voice of God and obey as his patriarch Noah had done in his day. This moment was not about race, outward looks, or even nationality. It was about overcoming deception to follow God into the ways of truth. It was with this decision that Abram broke away from "culture" to follow the One True God.

And Haran died before his father Terah in the land of his nativity, in Ur of the Chaldees. And Abram and Nahor took them wives: the name of Abram's wife [was] Sarai; and the name of Nahor's wife, Milcah, the daughter of Haran, the father of Milcah, and the father of Iscah. But Sarai was barren; she [had] no child. And Terah took Abram his son, and Lot the son of Haran his son's son, and Sarai his daughter in law, his son Abram's wife; and they went forth with them from Ur of the Chaldees, to go into the land of Canaan; and they came unto Haran, and dwelt there. And the days of Terah were two hundred and five years: and Terah died in Haran.
Genesis 11:28-32

And Joshua said unto all the people, Thus saith the LORD God of Israel, Your fathers dwelt on the other side of the flood in old time, [even] Terah, the father of Abraham, and the father of Nachor: and they served other gods.
Joshua 24:2

To understand the obstacles Abram faced, one would have to understand the ways of the Chaldeans. The Chaldeans worked to develop a unique ethnic identity and they eventually found it in the formation of Babylon.

Babylon was formed out of the character of the men who established it. The Chaldeans were famous for their warrior qualities and terrorism. They were rebellious and found themselves worshipping many gods. Historically speaking, societies tend to find themselves creating gods that agree with the natures of the men in charge as a substitute for acknowledging the True Creator. Many societies make gods out of their leaders. And so it was in the days of Babylon. While Abram was a Chaldea by birth, inside he was compelled to seek righteousness and follow the ways of the God who created heaven and earth. God specifically gave Abram a command to leave a man-made culture and ethos and follow Him.

Now the LORD had said unto Abram, Get thee out of thy country, and from thy kindred, and from thy father's house, unto a land that I will shew thee: And I will make of thee a great nation, and I will bless thee, and make thy name great; and thou shalt be a blessing: And I will bless them that bless thee, and curse him that curseth thee: and in thee shall all families of the earth be blessed.
Genesis 12:1-2

Out of a single man's obedience, a new start would begin. Abram would be called upon to have a change of focus. Instead of focusing on the destitute condition of

38

his man-made surroundings, on the propagation of his superior racial progeny, or the exaltation of his ancestry, he listened to the internal voice of God leading him on a journey that compelled him to be God-focused. This moved him from seeking an external, carnal existence with stone, wood, and gold, to an internal existence that seeks a personal and interactive relationship with God Himself. It was here that God called out to Abram to take a path that would deliver him from a fallen existence. As he obeyed God, he developed purpose, character, and wisdom as he denied his selfish nature and let God guide and correct him. His existence was transformed from society's established norms to a discovery of God's intentions for all people. Abram was one step away from a journey that would transform him into another man. This moment was crucial because his name, Abram, denoted an existence that further exalted his nationality, his father's teachings, and even his father's ways. Abram means, "my father is exalted." To change his future required a change in his purpose, which we see signified by his name. To change his purpose required a change of character through a relationship with God.

Not only would this moment change Abram, but it would define the bold existence of those who would follow him in pursuit of God. The voice of God spoke and told Abram about a great nation that would result from his obedience. This nation was not to be born out of any particular race, or even a single, family lineage. It would be a nation born from a relationship with God and defined by the internal leading of God. The biological generations that proceeded from Abram's loins failed to realize the importance of this relationship and proclaimed ownership and birthright to the privilege of God's favor as a genetic trait. But this text reveals that such a right can only be obtained from within. The Hebrew word for, "great nation," implies a people twisted together, loud in sound, committed in intensity; a people important to God. It would not be a chosen faction. It would be a people gathered from all races of the earth, united as one family through common faith and intensity of pursuit toward God. It would be conceived within homes and within groups that would seek and follow the Lord and His ways of righteousness. Like Abram had no way of making choices for his family lineage before him, he also had no way of seeing the choices of those who would come after him. While failure was sure to follow in some, and wickedness was sure to be a heavy influence on others, God was speaking of all those who would be unified by a desire to know the God who birthed His creation with plan and purpose.

And in thy seed shall all the nations of the earth be blessed; because thou hast obeyed my voice.
Genesis 22:18

And the scripture, foreseeing that God would justified the heathen through faith, preached before the gospel unto Abraham, [saying], In thee shall all nations be blessed.
Galatians 3:8

The varied beliefs of ethos and the cultures developed out of humanistic sin nature will always be divisive. God called Abram. But after Abram turned away from his pagan culture and ethos, God changed his purpose, destiny, and name to Abraham, "the father of a multitude." It was to Abraham that God made the promise. It was Abraham, the servant and friend of God, that God promised to make a blessing to the nations. God cannot bless those who glorify their culture above their pursuit of Him. God promised to bring people together out of every nation, tribe, and tongue who would operate, not by the external divisions and cultural limitations of their respective societies, but out of a unified heart to seek what is right according to God's purpose from the beginning. The fallen nature within man never disqualifies the original purposes of God toward mankind. His purpose has always been the inward relationship with us to teach us His ways so we can experience His blessing in a broken world.

Without His purpose as our goal, we are ignorant of our failures, gratify our fallen nature, become bankrupt in our character, and justify our own wickedness. We find ourselves gathering with those who feel the same. We become convinced that another group of humanity is responsible for our sufferings and failures. Our short-sightedness causes us to blame each other for the pain we perpetuate through bitterness and self-destructive habits. We fail to acknowledge our own faults and become blind to the true causes of our deteriorating conditions. The fallen nature reaches for help by going to external things to bring gratification or vindication in the pain. We seek relief through the lust of the flesh, the lust of the eyes, and the pride of life, only to cause ourselves more destruction. This is the cycle initiated by the fall: pain is caused by sin; relief of pain is expected through more sin; destruction grows into endless death. This causes division, blame, and hate for one another as external things become the focus. But external things can never bring resolve to a pain that comes from internal deficiency.

The internal leading of God leads us to the blessing with no ulterior motive. This is peculiar from the systems of the world because sinful nature traps us in conflicting motives. To be led by God is to make God the focus so that when failure comes, we continue to be filled with God's love and overcome it. Failure will inevitably arise from within.

When we fail, the only healing method is to repent to God and to those we injured so that we can see God clearly again and be led to what is right. Those who desire this seem strange to the world. But the people who seek God and His ways desire all people to be restored. When individuals fail to follow God in a true relationship, the fallen nature spreads throughout all institutions. This nature can be found in nations, governments, businesses, religions, schools, families, and homes. It lives inside of all races of people. The desire to be restored to God is the only way for people to be healed and truly care about the treatment of others. Apart from God, no nationality will ever heal because it is His Spirit that restores a man from the inside out.

For thou [art] an holy people unto the LORD thy God, and the LORD hath chosen thee to be a peculiar people unto himself, above all the nations that [are] upon the earth.
Deuteronomy 14:2

But ye [are] a chosen generation, a royal priesthood, an holy nation, a peculiar people; that ye should shew forth the praises of him who hath called you out of darkness into his marvellous light: Which in time past [were] not a people, but [are] now the people of God: which had not obtained mercy, but now have obtained mercy.
1 Peter 2:9-10

The Nation of the Name

When any nation forgets the ways of God or fails to acknowledge the Creator, they necessarily find themselves replacing God with beliefs and standards that men have created. If the nation is not "under God," then the nation is under the prevailing influence of man. In a tyranny, the nation is subjugated and obeys the dictates of one evil man. In an oligarchy, it obeys a group of evil men. In a democracy, it obeys the majority of evil men. A republic is unique because it tries to limit the influence of evil men by making it difficult for them to obtain power in each sphere of government. The demise of the republic occurs when most of the people you must choose from to fill the governing bodies are evil. The flaw then is not with the government - it has become a deeper problem relating to the character of the populace. If the influence of evil men is responsible for the downfall of a nation, we begin to understand that the influence an authority is under has the power to heal a nation or to destroy it. Therefore, God's ruling over mankind is of utmost importance. While all people will find themselves inadequate from time to time, not all will submit their inadequacies and fallen nature to the scrutiny of God's standard. This relegates mankind to the absolute impossibility of trying to heal themselves. In their futile efforts, they are led to false gods that influence their thinking and only make things worse.

History bears record that men separated from God produce chaos. When I speak of God, I am not speaking of the mere ritual or religion. People fail to realize that practicing outward acts cannot cure internal corruption in character. The inward nature of man must submit to the plans and purposes of God if there is to be true and lasting change. When corrupt governments promote change, they tend to force social conformity to predetermined humanistic ideals. They develop systems that are driven by a class of self-appointed elites that work to rid the multitudes of awareness and allegiance to God. The goal is to erase God so no one feels guilt or conviction through pricking in the conscience. They force people who seek God to infallibly prove or else deny the truths exhibited in creation. By doing this, they rid society of anyone speaking righteousness. No one can escape sin's destitution or be an example of God's character and righteousness when there is no one left to demonstrate the truth He teaches. Worldly government cannot help but pervert national, social, and cultural beliefs and force everyone to conform. Those who will not conform are eventually brutalized and exterminated.

46

In such instances, individual rights are taken away and the wicked masses are so unified that they become convinced that they are doing the right thing. The so-called right thing is determined by the people in power at the time, yet it is ever-changing because there is no standard of truth without God.

In every nation, people come together for different reasons. Some nations are founded on the acquisition of material or wealth, others gather simply because of the attributes of a natural location. Some start in a location because of the abundance of food. Others with the idea of conquest that leads to fame. When you look at the founding of the nations of the earth, you find many inspirations like these written into the names of the nations. It seems that fallen man is always stimulated by the acquisition of outward things such as land, riches, power over people, minerals, industry, or even war. The idea of conquest demonstrates the lust of man. It is never satisfied and always tries to feed itself. It is willing to destroy, steal, and kill to try to satisfy itself. The fallen nature thinks it is god and can break creation's rules to fulfill its driving need of ambition and desire. In all its efforts, satisfaction never comes, and pain and destruction lay in its wake. Man turns and justifies self by pointing a sin-ridden finger at God and declaring that He is the source of pain and destruction. With self at stake, they never come to the real conclusion that, apart from God and His ways, humans use their creative power in slavery to wickedness and produce nothing but a mess.

While God demonstrates His creative power in the various characteristics of racial features and the principle of individuality, He does not go to the externals to determine His outlook. While God says that His creation is good, and even very good at the six days of creation, we find that He planned to place it in the hands of creative man so that it would be cared for in His order. God's plan was not creation for creation's sake. It was God's desire to dwell with mankind as he enjoyed all of creation. When God looks at people across the globe, He always starts His search from within. His greatest desire is that people would make Him the intent of their heart. But since the fall, outward acquisition and the gratification of lust seem to be the order of the world. This is why evil spirits influence the minds of men. They are trying to unify a new world order, one in which all people are controlled by a single world system using all the natural resources to keep mankind apart from God's plan of internal union.

For the earnest expectation of the creature waiteth for the manifestation of the sons of God. For the creature was made subject to vanity, not willingly, but by reason of him who hath subjected [the same] in hope, Because the creature itself also shall be delivered from the bondage of corruption into the glorious liberty of the children of God. For we know that the whole creation groaneth and travaileth in pain together until now. And not only [they], but ourselves also, which have the firstfruits of the Spirit, even we ourselves groan within ourselves, waiting for the adoption, [to wit], the redemption of our body.

Romans 8:19-23

While the nations of the earth and various global corporations advance in the agenda of power and control, creation itself longs to be in the hands of those who desire God's purposes. Instead of giving into the lustful, power-hungry, fallen nature, God is at work in the hearts of people around the globe that seek an inward relationship with Him. This inward relationship with God instills a desire to seek ways that are right and correct, fulfilling the will of nature's God as He created it. As we have written in previous chapters, the desire to seek God internally is a desire to be a person of the right character and purpose. This is what it means to be a son or daughter of God. The systems of the world rule by stimulating the lust and pain of people who think life is all about the externals. They divide faction against faction, race against race, pain against pain. Politicians decide which issue is going to be on the agenda of the day based on who elects them to office and make boastful proclamations that man-made government is the answer.

These very governments use division as a means of control. God is not the divisive force among humanity. The divisive force comes through the sinful nature as it yields to the influence and imaginations of other spirits. The whole goal of the fallen world system is to keep humanity from having a heartfelt relationship with God. While God is the Creator and demonstrates His power through the diversity of races, He does not use race like the demonic world systems and governments. He unifies His people in a different way. The nations of the earth try to unify people by biological flesh or systems of ethnicity and culture. God unifies His people by the righteousness and character that flows from within.

Then Peter opened [his] mouth, and said, Of a truth I perceive that God is no respecter of persons: But in

every nation he that feareth him, and worketh
righteousness, is accepted with him.
Acts 10:34-35

The methods of the world seem to revolve around forcing people into groups based on outward appearance or by unifying people by the fallen nature of the flesh. God bypasses both methods and starts working on a man from the inward character, molding him to do what is right. When we realize this, we discover the journey for us to understand what a child of God is. While the KJV translation often uses the word, "sons," in the Greek, we find the word "teknon" which is defined as offspring or children. This word shows us that God intends to be the Father of all those who allow Him to govern their lives from within. My understanding of this word leads me to the conclusion that the children of God are the flesh, the bodies, that God flows through. They are those who seek to use their bodies to maintain His purposes in a broken world. People who are seeking God, His ways, and His will, desire to walk with Him and be His ambassadors in the earth.

Behold, what manner of love the Father hath bestowed
upon us, that we should be called the sons of God:

51

therefore the world knoweth us not, because it knew him not. Beloved, now are we the sons of God, and it doth not yet appear what we shall be: but we know that, when he shall appear, we shall be like him; for we shall see him as he is.
1 John 3:1-2

For as many as are led by the Spirit of God, they are the sons of God.
Romans 8:14

That ye may be blameless and harmless, the sons of God, without rebuke, in the midst of a crooked and perverse nation, among whom ye shine as lights in the world; holding forth the Word of life.
Philippians 2:15-16

This understanding of the "sons" of God may seem new to many of you reading this chapter, but I affirm to you that it goes back to Adam himself. Even though Adam and Eve activated the fallen nature, they never lost their ability to choose to commune with God and follow His direction. Their relationship with God continued once they answered His call to come out from behind the trees. It was then that they learned the consequences of their action. God only desired for them to know "good." But now they would have to learn to partake in the consequence of knowing evil. They found out that they would have to rule over themselves in a battle against Satan while being inflicted with pain, hardship, and toil. God would take sinless animals and cover them as a symbol of His desire to remain in a relationship with them, even though they had disobeyed. During that moment, Adam and Eve chose to obey God's instructions and continue in their relationship so they could follow His ways. The effect of this choice is revealed in the genealogy of Jesus as it is written in Luke.

Which was the son of Enos, which was the son of Seth, which was the son of Adam, which was the son of God.
Luke 3:38

As you know, Adam and Eve initially gave birth to two sons. In the story of Cain and Able, we see two individuals with two different natures. As children, they would have been taught the ways of God and gained an understanding of the blood sacrifice and the benefits of obedience to Father God. They had learned that the greatest qualification to a relationship with God was heartfelt obedience. Somewhere along the way, Cain

53

moved from an internal heart of obedience to yielding to the sinful nature of rebellion that wanted his way of doing things. In Cain, we see a son who refused to heed the voice of God and acted out of his fallen nature. He murdered his brother and left God's presence. Being led by his selfish ambitions, Cain would soon create a lineage of lust-filled people. They set up cities, world governments, and industries. They worked through murder, greed, paganism, and demonic culture, and loved the feeling of power and the fleshly gratification of sin. This would come to be known as the lineage of man.

While the lineage of Cain multiplied, God continued to work with Adam to produce a people after His heart on the earth. In God's restorative plan, we find that God allowed Adam and Eve to bring forth another son who would follow God and produce a lineage of people who would seek God and honor Him from the heart.

And Adam knew his wife again; and she bare a son, and called his name Seth: For God, [said she], hath appointed me another seed instead of Abel, whom Cain slew. And to Seth, to him also there was born a son; and he called his name Enos: then began men to call upon the name of the LORD.
Genesis 4:25-26

The Sons of God would be those who had an internal cry to fulfill God's purposes and a heart relationship with God Himself. It was Seth and his lineage that sought the Lord. They wanted to bear His name and fulfill His purpose on the earth. The Hebrew word for "name" is transliterated "sem." Sem means, "one's reputation, character, renown, and report." In essence, these men wanted to represent God. They desired to carry God's likeness and represent His character rather than the self-centered nature manifested by fallen man. God had compensated for the loss of Able by bringing forth a lineage that would serve Him and multiply His character and ways in the earth.

This [is] the book of the generations of Adam. In the day that God created man, in the likeness of God made he him; Male and female created he them; and blessed them, and called their name Adam, in the day when they were created. And Adam lived an hundred and thirty years, and begat a son in his own likeness, after his image; and called his name Seth
Genesis 5:1-3

When God made Adam and Eve, He made them in His likeness and image. God's likeness and image is Spirit, and it is the spirit created within man that allows man to hear from God internally. When mankind fell, it introduced man to evil and instilled a nature of lust and pride. However, the Spirit of God touches the internal spirit of man, speaking through the conscience, and calls out to man to be restored to God. While Cain chose to leave the presence of the Lord, Seth remained faithful and desired to bear the image of God throughout His life. These two opposing desires reveal the heart and cause a clash between societies, but first, this clash is faced from within. The fallen man wants to rule the world, thereby gratifying external lust. The son of God desires to bring forth God's will and seeks to restore His creation principles. While all men feel the effects of the fall, many will choose to follow God's plans over the corrupt nature within their flesh. Those who make this choice and desire a true relationship with God will seek Him and be used in their generation.

In an earlier chapter, we discovered that after the flood Noah's sons were called upon to repopulate the earth. In Noah's days, sin had spread so rampant that Noah was the only man who was in a relationship with God. The lineage of Cain had not only perverted society, but it had even perverted the sons of God through the work of the carnal desires and sexual lust.

And it came to pass, when men began to multiply on the face of the earth, and daughters were born unto them, That the sons of God saw the daughters of men that they [were] fair; and they took them wives of all which they chose.

Genesis 6:1-2

As people move farther from the Lord, the influence of lust turns them over to weakness. Perversion takes over, leaving whole nations and cities consumed by evil. When evil pervades a society, it proceeds to drown out the voice of God by silencing those who are seeking righteousness. By the time we get to Genesis 11 and the tower of Babel, we see that all men came together speaking the same language. It is a language of perversion, a language of selfishness, a language of greed, self-centeredness, and power. In this way, the one world spirit unifies its followers, and they fail to see that they are being led to destruction. With righteousness silenced, whole generations can be born into a world that is automatically perverse. Perversion becomes the norm and people move farther from God and closer to annihilation. While the tower of Babel represents the gathering of the fallen world, the second half of Genesis 11 shows the genealogy of Shem. This genealogy stands in direct opposition to the onslaught of demonic unity gathering in society. Earlier, we discovered that Shem was the son of Noah who had a completely distinctive character. His name means, "the bearer of the name." In correlation with the previous words we investigated, this would mean that Shem and his lineage would continue the lineage of the sons of God. They would seek to bear God's character, nature, and image on the earth while most of the populace would give over to the nature of the flesh.

These [are] the generations of Shem: Shem [was] an hundred years old, and begat Arphaxad two years after the flood: ... Now these [are] the generations of Terah: Terah begat Abram, Nahor, and Haran; and Haran begat Lot.
Genesis 11:10, 27

In Shem's genealogy, we see a recurring theme in the names. Their name meanings represent a group of people separated from the world and growing in God. It is a picture of the sons of God growing step by step to fulfill

58

God's plans. By the time we get to Terah, we see that society had interfered with the Sons of God. Terah's name means "delayed." While Terah was in the lineage of the Name and had been taught about it, historical writings say he served false gods and delayed God's plans. The historical book of Jasher documents and explains the great delay that Terah faced. He found himself in the service of Nimrod, the king of Babel, as a government official. His society suffered a pervasive influence of hedonism which altered Terah's thinking and beliefs. As this historical account plays out, we find that Abram had been living in the house of Noah. If we do the math from the genealogy contained in Genesis 11, Noah would have been 892 years old at the time Abram was born. Since Noah lived to be 950 years old, he would have lived for 58 years after Abram was born. Therefore, it could be accurate that Abram was taught by him and dwelled in his home. Abram finds his father and confronts him. This confrontation leads to a dispute with Nimrod concerning the worship of man-made idols. In essence, Abram stood toe to toe with the anti-Christ government system in his day. This confrontation not only established Abram in his beliefs, but it set him on a journey with God that would unify people around the world for the rest of time. Abram would not only end the delay of God's plan and seek the name of the Lord, but his walk with God would also cause his name to change. This name change would be so powerful that his lineage would go beyond the natural bloodline and gather people together from all the nations of the earth.

God made this the start of a new nation. He would also establish the process of character change, from the cry of an inward heart to the revealing of external character. This idea of seeking God's character would take Abram and make him Abraham. Sarai would become Sarah. Jacob would change to Israel, Simeon to Peter, and Saul to Paul. Seeking the Name of the Lord would become the core factor of differentiating God's people from the people of the world, who always seek their own name. The ways of the world unify people by perversion, sin, and lust. Its systems try to identify people by nationality, race, and social status. To be a part of God's plans we must accept that God has a plan that is beyond the fallen system.

It does not take much to participate in the ideals and beliefs of the world. For people to be led by their weakness and lust filled flesh, all they must do is live in it. The state of sin is natural to people whose only reality is sin and whose desire is to gratify and preserve the carnal. The result of a nation led in this way is only destruction, wickedness, slavery to manmade government, plague, ruin, and death. Of course, sin-filled people blame one another for the negative results. They point their finger of blame at a nationality, social class, political party, or people group. Truth be told, sin is the culprit. People living outside of God's order and plan will bring the breakdown of any society. If hearts do not turn and repent, it will be the righteous that are scorned because they believe in a God of standards. In the United States of America, people choose their political servants. Therefore, people are responsible for choosing wicked leaders that give them the promise of security through monetary benefits. A populace, blind to their inexorable wickedness, gropes in blindness when it goes to vote for the leader that offers them wicked desires without God's boundaries.

All it takes for a nation and its people to change course is for them to acknowledge their wickedness and turn and seek the Lord. As individuals choose to seek God and call upon His name, a relationship with God develops, yielding great benefits. Salvation, redemption of sin, and even signs, wonders, and miracles occur for those who will take a stand and be led by the Holy Spirit. Being Holy Spirit led brings God's goodness into the earth.

61

The LORD bless thee, and keep thee: The LORD make his face shine upon thee, and be gracious unto thee: The LORD lift up his countenance upon thee, and give thee peace. And they shall put my name upon the children of Israel; and I will bless them.
Numbers 6:24-27

And I will shew wonders in heaven above, and signs in the earth beneath; blood, and fire, and vapour of smoke: The sun shall be turned into darkness, and the moon into blood, before that great and notable day of the Lord come: And it shall come to pass, [that] whosoever shall call on the name of the Lord shall be saved.
Acts 2:19-21

Our help [is] in the name of the LORD, who made heaven and earth.
Psalm 124:8

The name of the LORD [is] a strong tower: the righteous runneth into it, and is safe.
Proverbs 18:10

Help us, O God of our salvation, for the glory of thy name: and deliver us, and purge away our sins, for thy name's sake.

Psalm 79:9

O Lord, hear; O Lord, forgive; O Lord, hearken and do; defer not, for thine own sake, O my God: for thy city and thy people are called by thy name.

Daniel 9:19

Their Redeemer [is] strong; the LORD of hosts [is] his name: he shall thoroughly plead their cause, that he may give rest to the land, and disquiet the inhabitants of Babylon.

Jeremiah 50:34

Neither is there salvation in any other: for there is none other name under heaven given among men, whereby we must be saved.

Acts 4:12

I ask you, as an individual, to recognize the power of the world's influence over your thinking and life. Instead of becoming a part of the pain and problem by believing the lies indoctrinating you through manmade deceit,

63

submit your life and breathe back to the God that formed you. He is a God who uniquely unifies His people. Nations of the earth try to unify people by biological flesh or systems of ethnicity and culture. In their efforts, they break down people and leave them feeling alone and alienated. Evil leaders depend on the people's ignorance of God so they will not recognize their loss of God-given freedom, rights, and home.

Join those seeking God. Be joined with another people, seeking another city and another country - one whose builder and Maker is God. He alone has the power to satisfy humanity. God has always been about people who are unified by righteousness and character that flows from the inside. It is the internal that cries out in you that seeks something beyond the divisiveness of evil man. God is unifying His nation by restoring those who seek after and trust in His name.

But as many as received him, to them gave he power to become the sons of God, [even] to them that believe on his name:
John 1:1

Spread Among Nations

Under God's system of government, there is accountability. His spheres of jurisdiction center on the individual and end up with the Nation. He investigates the heart and invites people to be a part of His plans. When people reject Him, He allows them their free choice to follow their lust and be influenced by the false beliefs of a realm that will destroy them and the intent of God's creation. As the dark influences increase, the people of God can be influenced as well. They can develop mixed beliefs and fail to make God their only source. When this happens, God reaches out. But the hearts of his people wain as they reach for other loves. At the start of their relationship, people reach out to God as the creator to help them build good things on the earth. However, as their hearts divide, they become conflicted about their source and glorify man and self as the builder of it all. When people believe the narratives of worldly society and accept the influence of demonically inspired philosophies, they become spiritually weak and are easily taken advantage of. Over time, they stop trusting completely on God. Satan takes advantage of this failure and condemns their guilt-ridden conscience, discouraging them from returning to God. In

65

this way, people begin to feel their only option is to join the world in using substances and perversion to try to numb the pain. As this subjugation becomes pervasive, their unnatural state of corruption begins to appear normal, to the point people fail to realize that the pain they feel is a result of running away from God. The worldly governments rejoice as the people become weak and dependent. Believing they have no source to help them, people grovel to sinful men in an antichrist state system.

Instead of returning to God as their only source, people begin to chant the name of their false gods. For some, this is a political party. For others, it is a social justice group, a preferred chemical addiction, a specific gratification of the flesh, a corporation, an amassing of wealth, or even the supposed power of their nation itself. All these sources are limited in power, leading their followers to destruction instead of restoration. God looks for a people to serve Him. But many times, people are deceived about the purity of their hearts concerning God. Deception can be so strong that people who were formerly committed to God, continue to hold his name in their mouth after their heart pursuit leads them where God never intended them to go.

And they come unto thee as the people cometh, and they sit before thee as my people, and they hear thy words, but they will not do them: for with their mouth they shew much love, [but] their heart goeth after their covetousness.
Ezekiel 33:31

People who practice religion repeat external works and rituals in an attempt to cleanse their conscience of feelings of guilt concerning internal lusts and idolatry (literal and figurative) instead of allowing the internal relationship with God to cleanse the motives and thereby change the external behaviors. In this event, people become split into factions based on which denomination, religion, or church organization will pronounce them righteous. Sunday mornings are the most racially segregated time in America. Denominationalism keeps people comfortable with their limitations. People vote for the Jesus they want to be preached as the offering plate goes by, withholding their support if the preacher gets too holy or calls too many prayer services. On the other side, corrupt clergy manipulate Scripture to appeal to the feelings of their congregation, using the offering as validation that they are "giving the people what they need." They base their topics on social status and the financial and moral condition of the people they serve instead of being led by God to equip them with knowledge and wisdom to instruct the congregation on how to manage all of life's situations. Many church groups use specific texts to reinforce the covert philosophy of the world hiding in their belief system. This results in the people feeling trapped in their specific situation. The problem with believing and trusting in the world is that it drives people to a human to fix the problem. Instead of laying hold of Godly responses to the situation, wrong beliefs are strengthened, and people become more firmly snared in their destitute condition of life. Of course, the world reinforces these views. They call it compassion to validate the sin that hurts people while attacking people who offer truth and relief from the mental and spiritual prison.

It may seem like simple ignorance. Unfortunately, it is not so innocent. They know that, when people are healed and leave a state of desperation, it becomes difficult to make a profit from them. Desperate people make bad decisions and will turn to anything for relief. Man-based programs keep the systems of desperation in place, make the world of destruction go round, and guarantee those involved in controlling the means of relief a steady monetary gain. God is the only source that people can go to that not only relieves the pain but also corrects the deficiency that caused it in the first place.

Previously, we stated that, for the external to change, the internal desire and belief must change. Since the fall, people have been trained to depend on their carnal minds to sustain an earthly existence. Without proper training from God, we operate in limitation, believing this world is all there is. We live only to satisfy the outside, instead of following God from the inside. Believing that external gratification is the reason for our existence, our lusts fight for limited resources. As a result, our world is divided as people groups fight over humanity's broken scraps. This cycle repeats until subjugation becomes the standard of existence. It is not shocking that the sinful world has flawed beliefs and operates in a carnal existence. For those who long to follow God, the Creator, lust is replaced by the depth of our relationship with God internally. We serve a God who overcomes every obstacle. If God can overcome Pharoah, topple nations and bring down armies, feed the multitudes and keep the shoes on our feet, surely, He can correct racism, overcome social status, break poverty, and deliver those who desire Him. The problem is not God. It is finding a willing people that will seek Him and His ways.

When religious practice is taught, people stop following God and start associating God with a certain group or race of people. Religion and culture teach us to identify people exclusively by race or status instead of seeing that people have the potential to be used by God. They try to use the outward to identify who has a heart towards God. In the Old Testament, we find that the significance of being Jewish became more important to the descendants of Abraham than following God Himself. Being born into Abraham's bloodline meant that you were certainly one of the chosen and were somehow special and set apart. Eventually, this mindset caused the Jews to sow racism. It caused them to disparage certain people groups based on their inferior national identity. Therefore, being Jewish became more about practicing the rituals than the pursuit of an inner relationship with God. Misinformed descendants looked to outward circumcision to prove who they were instead of to the God who holds all our identities in His hand.

Biologically, Abram was not born a Jew. He *became* one. He was a Chaldea. It was his belief, not his race or nationality, that started his process of transformation.

And he believed in the LORD; and he counted it to him for righteousness. And he said unto him, I [am]

70

the LORD that brought thee out of Ur of the
Chaldees, to give thee this land to inherit it.
Genesis 15:6-7

Abram chose to follow God and God chose to have a relationship with Abram. That is what caused his descendants to reap great results, but only if they would continue to seek the Lord. Racism was not involved in God's choice. We find that the descendants of Abraham would be gathered from many nations, tribes, and people. Race, nationality, social status, and ritual religion would not be the common denominator of the people God would call.

Long before "Jew" existed as a race or nationality, the word, "Hebrew," would come into use. The word, "Hebrew," is defined as, "one from beyond or from another region." As Abram traveled with God, he met many people groups. For the first time, many people would hear about the One True Living God. At that time, people had been indoctrinated in the ways of the world through the same spirits that ruled the descendants of Cain. When Abraham walked among the people, he would be classified as an outsider or someone from a distant land. The moniker of "Hebrew" did not start with just Abraham. It was associated with all the descendants of Shem as, "the people of the name." This word was identified as "Eber" before it was assigned an identity of race or class of people.

Unto Shem also, the father of all the children of Eber, the brother of Japheth the elder, even to him were [children] born.
Genesis 10:21

And there came one that had escaped, and told Abram the Hebrew; for he dwelt in the plain of Mamre the Amorite, brother of Eshcol, and brother of Aner: and these [were] confederate with Abram.
Genesis 14:13

In a world of paganism and worldly governments, Abram was sent forth and identified as an outsider. He was one unknown to or a part of the world system or culture. During his travels, many were called to his side, and many walked with him in covenant relationship, even while his identity was being established. The nations of the earth noticed a significant difference between the gods of the earth and the One True God of Abraham. One of the greatest factors that distinguished Abraham and his descendants from all the other cultures was that he worshipped a God that could not be seen but could be heard by those who followed Him. The followers of this God eventually became known as Jews. But this word still does not find its use in the context of standard racial identity, but rather in the unseen quality of the God they worshipped. The word, "Jew," is a derivative of the name of one of Abraham's descendants whose name is Judah. "Judah" means, "the one who praises Jah." It comes from the root word "Yada," which means one who throws the hands up and thanks God, this causes God to show His hand of strength and power.

And she conceived again, and bare a son: and she said, Now will I praise the LORD: therefore she called his name Judah; and left bearing.
Genesis 29:35

The pagan nations of the earth were all about war. It is within the fallen nature to destroy, and the demonic influence through paganism is always out to murder. As the followers of God increase through Abraham's descendants, inevitably, the dark world wages a spiritual battle that reveals itself in the natural. Time after time, the Jewish nation would be identified with the praises out in front of the battle. God came to the aid of his people and the reputation of the One True God would spread as He honored His relationship with his people. The demonic gods glory in all types of destruction. Under their influence, the sin nature within man is stimulated and a never-ending pursuit of power, greed, and lust ensues. Insomuch as God's people would put Him first, the battle against the carnal army would turn. Before tradition converted the word Jew to represent a nationality, it was first a condition of the heart.

The power of God that brings change to a person is the first step in changing a group of people or a nation. When God chose Abram and changed him to Abraham, He was making a declaration of the impact a single person could have by showing people the result of responding to the opportunity of allowing God to change their lives. Many people fail to understand this impact and qualify a person's goodness based on being born into a certain family or race, or even by being a part of a political party or nation. The truth is, we are just being partial to the group with which we are associated. When it comes to family association, people group, race, religion, or any other gathering of people, many of us make overreaching comments trying to make whole groups inclusive. God is not like this. He takes people one at a time. Walking with God is not something passed down to our natural descendants. It is something to be pursued.

This brings us to the story of Esau and Jacob. Early on, the heart of Esau was revealed when he made a legal sale of his birthright for a bowl of beans. This transaction displayed that his present carnal existence was of primary value to him in his life. Before Jacob sets out to steal Esau's spiritual blessing, we find that its transfer was already a completely legal transaction between him and his older brother. Legality is never the ultimate decision-maker concerning the motive of the heart. Jacob was not free from the carnal nature either. He was willing to lie and deceive to get the carnal things associated with the blessing and the birthright. I am reminded of how many people seek God for the physical prosperity instead of a personal change of heart. In Genesis 32, we read about Jacob's struggle to get the blessing from God. This represents a struggle with the lust of man's fallen nature that must yield to God. While it appears in some translations that Jacob won, his name tells something else. He is given the name, "Israel," which means, "God prevails" or "God's power strengthens." Once God wins, God changes his name to Israel. In Scripture, Jacob asks God for His name. This act signifies a longing for God's character and nature. Upon this request, the blessing is pronounced. While the character of Jacob was changed, the outward man was left with a limp to remind all of humanity that the fallen nature will always slow you down.

And he said, Thy name shall be called no more Jacob, but Israel: for as a prince hast thou power with God and with men, and hast prevailed. And Jacob asked [him], and said, Tell [me], I pray thee, thy name. And he said, Wherefore [is] it [that] thou dost ask after my name? And he blessed him there.
Genesis 32:28-29

This event was documented to establish a precedent for all those who would join the people of God. True service to God requires each of us to go through an internal change. Internal change never diminishes the fact that we must face external difficulty in ourselves and in others. When it was time to bless His descendants, Israel declared that his name would be pronounced upon a whole nation. While the name, Israel, was taken for the name of the nation, it was always meant to point the way back to the Name of The One who is far greater.

The Messenger which redeemed me from all evil, bless the lads; and let my name be named on them, and the name of my fathers Abraham and Isaac; and let them grow into a multitude in the midst of the earth.
Genesis 48:16

The blessing which results from following God is not a genetic trait inherited with each successive generation. Every generation must make a personal choice to pursue a relationship with God for themselves. When people fail to seek God, a nation collectively finds itself in pursuit of the same carnal passions. Apart from God, man will put their faith in themselves and fulfill their personal lusts. The nation of Israel was no exception. All things prospered when God ruled the hearts of the individuals, governed the directions of the families, and ruled through the priests and the judges. But when Israel got their eyes off God's plans and started walking in the same plan as the nations of the earth, they turned from dependence on God and asked for a man-made government to fight their battles. Abraham's descendants digressed from God's government as He was progressively ejected from the hearts of the people to being relegated to the tabernacle, and finally ousted from the government. When He was no longer allowed to rule, the people were no different than any other pagan nation. God cried out to them through the voice of the prophets. But, because He no longer ruled in their hearts, their carnal loves ruled the day.

Nevertheless the people refused to obey the voice of Samuel; and they said, Nay; but we will have a king over us; That we also may be like all the nations; and that our king may judge us, and go out before us, and fight our battles.
1 Samuel 8:19-20

And the children of Israel did evil in the sight of the LORD, and served Baalim: And they forsook the LORD God of their fathers, which brought them out of the land of Egypt, and followed other gods, of the gods of the people that [were] round about them, and bowed themselves unto them, and provoked the LORD to anger.
Judges 2:11-12

As Israel developed into a nation, it took on the characteristics of all the idolatry of the earth. Though they continued to practice external rituals, they found their confidence in their genealogy through Abraham, Isaac, and Jacob, instead of in a relationship with God Himself. God would send them messengers and prophets, yet they would not heed. Instead, they would murder the righteous and allow the people to choose their priests based on popularity or convenience. Though their hearts were far from God, they would constantly declare that they were God's chosen. In times of trouble, they would seek the Lord. But their hearts would continue to follow the lusts of the flesh. Priests and politicians pursued positions of power, motivated to oversee the law and purse. They reveled in self-indulged power to destroy some and exonerate others. In this way, they made themselves god and opened themselves up to fulfill the works of the devil. They became proud of their association with those who pursued God while rejecting a relationship with Him for themselves. They became heathen, and their response to God was based on tradition instead of a pure desire in the heart. They had a lingering perception of God but refused to grow their relationship and remained determined to continue in their wicked ways. In time, they underestimated the ramifications of the fact that a covenant relationship with God is two-sided.

For thou [art] an holy people unto the LORD thy God: the LORD thy God hath chosen thee to be a special people unto himself, above all people that [are] upon the face of the earth.
Deuteronomy 7:6

Relationship is the key that allows you to grow in God. If you are not growing in God, the other nature will surely overtake you. The word for, "chosen," is, "bahar," in Hebrew. It means, "to choose, to try, to examine, to see," often implying proving whether you will align with God and choose His ways. To be chosen by God, you must be willing to examine your own heart and choose His ways over your own. It is this examination of heart that identifies you as fulfilling God's will and not your own. You must choose His will over your ways. When we fail to walk His path, all He requires is for us to come to Him and acknowledge the failure, setting our hearts to seek Him again.

If they shall confess their iniquity, and the iniquity of their fathers, with their trespass which they trespassed against me, and that also they have walked contrary unto me; And [that] I also have walked contrary unto them, and have brought them into the land of their enemies; if then their uncircumcised hearts be humbled, and they then accept of the punishment of their iniquity: Then will I remember my covenant with Jacob, and also my covenant with Isaac, and also my covenant with Abraham will I remember; and I will remember the land.
Leviticus 26:40-42

To say that God chooses a people by ethnicity, nationality, or some outward physical characteristic is as much of a farce as saying that you are Godly if you are circumcised. The practice of outward circumcision has its natural health benefits as far as spreading infection during a moment of creation. But its spiritual implications reach much deeper. Circumcision is an external practice that represents the internal change that can happen when the sin nature is cut off from the heart. It was intended to be an outward sign of an inward work. In the spiritual context, the extra foreskin insinuated that the sin of the heart can spread and infect the natural world and make you less responsive to God's will. Those who desire God's blessing externally without the inward work of the heart are not true Jews. Their actions identify them as false.

Circumcise yourselves to the LORD, and take away the foreskins of your heart, ye men of Judah and inhabitants of Jerusalem: lest my fury come forth like fire, and burn that none can quench [it], because of the evil of your doings.
Jeremiah 4:4

Behold, the days come, saith the LORD, that I will punish all [them which are] circumcised with the uncircumcised; Egypt, and Judah, and Edom, and the children of Ammon, and Moab, and all [that are] in the utmost corners, that dwell in the wilderness: for all [these] nations [are] uncircumcised, and all the house of Israel [are] uncircumcised in the heart.
Jeremiah 9:25-26

For he is not a Jew, which is one outwardly; neither [is that] circumcision, which is outward in the flesh: But he [is] a Jew, which is one inwardly; and circumcision [is that] of the heart, in the spirit, [and] not in the letter; whose praise [is] not of men, but of God.
Romans 2:28-29

Therefore will I number you to the sword, and ye shall all bow down to the slaughter: because when I called, ye did not answer; when I spake, ye did not hear; but did evil before mine eyes, and did choose [that] wherein I delighted not.
Isaiah 65:12

The true intention of God for the descendants of Abraham was for the whole nation to be a kingdom of priests. They would carry His name throughout the earth and share the truth of the One True God. As the nation developed, they took on the patterns of the world and failed to deliver the truth of God to the other nations of the earth. It was never God's intention for His relational principles to stop with a certain race or nation. He saw all the descendants of Abraham as becoming a nation of people that would fulfill His will. The Jews took on the mindset that their chosen-ness was a result of being born to Abraham himself. They isolated themselves, huddling under the banner of a nationality. While God blessed the nation naturally, they failed to fulfill their spiritual mandate and began to use their status as a point of racism and national pride. Their own sin nature kept them from developing a relationship with God and they opposed His will by trying to conform God to their own exclusive group. This was never God's intent.

Now therefore, if ye will obey my voice indeed, and keep my covenant, then ye shall be a peculiar treasure unto me above all people: for all the earth [is] mine: And ye shall be unto me a kingdom of priests, and an holy nation. These [are] the words which thou shalt speak unto the children of Israel.
Exodus 19:5-6

After the nation of Israel failed to keep their God-given assignment, God, in His wisdom, allowed them to be scattered among all the nations of the earth. Not only was this a sign of His judgment, but it also allowed His name to be known throughout the world. People of all nations would hear of the One True God, even if His own people chose to reject His will and purpose. God is always in control. The exile caused Judaism to spread among all nations, all races, and all peoples. There are Jews among all the tribes of the earth to this day.

Many religions have employed this elitist mentality. Now many racial groups are declaring that they are the true Jews. They declare that they are from the ten missing tribes and assert that they are the true Jews. This declaration, in many cases, is out of a motivation for vengeance and a desire of retribution for the years sinful, racist men of other nationalities have mistreated them. Their pain runs so deep that they desire other races to be excluded from access to God. They desire for other nationalities to burn in hell, or they teach that the other nationalities will be their slaves in the afterlife. This is completely opposite of the heart of God. When God dispersed the people of Israel, He knew each heart, desiring to purge the wicked and leave those who would bear forth His name.

For, lo, I will command, and I will sift the house of Israel among all nations, like as [corn] is sifted in a sieve, yet shall not the least grain fall upon the earth. All the sinners of my people shall die by the sword, which say, The evil shall not overtake nor prevent us.
Amos 9:9-10

While He scattered the majority abroad, he left a remnant in the land he promised to Abraham, to bring about future restoration and fulfillment of prophecy. He

84

continues to use natural Israel as a sign and continues to fulfill His promise to them in a natural way, but He seeks to restore them spiritually as His desire is to all people.

And he carried away all Jerusalem, and all the princes, and all the mighty men of valour, [even] ten thousand captives, and all the craftsmen and smiths: none remained, save the poorest sort of the people of the land.
2 Kings 24:14

And he said, It is a light thing that thou shouldest be my servant to raise up the tribes of Jacob, and to restore the preserved of Israel: I will also give thee for a light to the Gentiles, that thou mayest be my salvation unto the end of the earth.
Isaiah 49:6

And their seed shall be known among the Gentiles, and their offspring among the people: all that see them shall acknowledge them, that they [are] the seed [which] the LORD hath blessed.
Isaiah 61:9

James, a servant of God and of the Lord Jesus Christ, to the twelve tribes which are scattered abroad, greeting.
James 1:1

God will see that His plans are fulfilled. He is God and His ways are far above any human or demonic intent. Ultimately, He offers all of humanity a choice to operate with Him. His name will be declared to the nations and the nations will choose who they will follow.

In the New Testament, Jesus's first ministry was to the lost sheep of Israel. While he desired to restore all men to God once and for all through His blood on the cross, as God in the flesh, He first wanted to be recognized by those who knew of Him so that they would resume the call to take His name to the nations of the earth. What He found was a people looking for a ruler to crush their enemies and gratify their carnal nature by establishing a physical government for themselves on the earth. The desire of God had never changed. From the first moment God walked with Abraham, to His coming into the world as a man, His desire was for all people. When He came, He maintained His original intent, which is to seek and save that which was lost. He had given his promise to Abraham. Restoration through Jesus Christ is the fulfillment of that promise and was offered first to the children of Abraham.

*But he answered and said, I am not sent but unto the
lost sheep of the house of Israel.*
Matthew 15:24

But go rather to the lost sheep of the house of Israel.
Matthew 10:6

*Hear the word of the LORD, O ye nations, and declare
[it] in the isles afar off, and say, He that scattered
Israel will gather him, and keep him, as a shepherd
[doth] his flock.*
Jeremiah 31:10

The problem Jesus encountered was that the people
He had called no longer recognized His voice. The
majority were busy fulfilling a lust-filled agenda. Their
purpose was no longer to seek after God, so blinded they
could not recognize the Messiah. They desired to be like
everyone else, running after a selfish carnality. While
God called out to many, He found but a few who would
hear Him. Yet those few would fulfill His purpose to the
uttermost once they learned obedience to the Father's
will. God is not a racist. He had declared his intentions
in the Old Testament, even before He took on the form
of man by entering a human body. Jesus. God in the
flesh would speak for Himself and would live a life that
exhibited the true heart of the Father towards people. He

gave a personal opportunity to even the most wicked among men. The Jews practiced racism and continued blind in the "chosen" mindset. Jesus touched people of every class and nation because God had never intended to exclude any race of people.

And the Gentiles shall see thy righteousness, and all kings thy glory: and thou shalt be called by a new name, which the mouth of the LORD shall name.
Isaiah 62:2

Also the sons of the stranger, that join themselves to the LORD, to serve him, and to love the name of the LORD, to be his servants, every one that keepeth the sabbath from polluting it, and taketh hold of my covenant; Even them will I bring to my holy mountain, and make them joyful in my house of prayer: their burnt offerings and their sacrifices [shall be] accepted upon mine altar; for mine house shall be called an house of prayer for all people. The Lord GOD which gathereth the outcasts of Israel saith, Yet will I gather [others] to him, beside those that are gathered unto him.
Isaiah 56:6-8

O LORD, my strength, and my fortress, and my refuge in the day of affliction, the Gentiles shall come unto thee from the ends of the earth, and shall say, Surely our fathers have inherited lies, vanity, and [things]

*wherein [there is] no profit. Shall a man make gods
unto himself, and they [are] no gods? Therefore,
behold, I will this once cause them to know, I will
cause them to know mine hand and my might; and they
shall know that my name [is] The LORD.*
Jeremiah 16:19-21

*For from the rising of the sun even unto the going
down of the same my name [shall be] great among the
Gentiles; and in every place incense [shall be] offered
unto my name, and a pure offering: for my name [shall
be] great among the heathen, saith the LORD of
hosts.*
Malachi 1:11

*Simeon hath declared how God at the first did visit the
Gentiles, to take out of them a people for his name.
And to this agree the words of the prophets; as it is
written, After this I will return, and will build again the
tabernacle of David, which is fallen down; and I will
build again the ruins thereof, and I will set it up: That
the residue of men might seek after the Lord, and all
the Gentiles, upon whom my name is called, saith the
Lord, who doeth all these things.*
Acts 15:14-17

Not only did God seek to restore His relationship by

walking and talking with the Jewish disciples and

touching people of other nations, but He also knew that

their racism would have to be overcome through the

work of His Spirit. It is only the power of the Spirit of God that can reveal the will of God to a carnal people. Jesus paid the price to atone for the sins of the world so that all people could return to Him. The Jewish religious system had been twisted by wicked men promoting nationalism and racism. The Jews tried to reserve access to God specifically for their chosen race or nationality. God knew that the Jewish law could not separate man from sin because of carnal limitations. He knew that it would take His power for man to fulfill His will and take His saving power to the world. He did not want His power limited by any racial barrier. So, He gives us Acts Chapter 2.

And when the day of Pentecost was fully come, they were all with one accord in one place. And suddenly there came a sound from heaven as of a rushing mighty wind, and it filled all the house where they were sitting. And there appeared unto them cloven tongues like as of fire, and it sat upon each of them. And they were all filled with the Holy Ghost, and began to speak with other tongues, as the Spirit gave them utterance. And there were dwelling at Jerusalem Jews, devout men, out of every nation under heaven. Now when this was noised abroad, the multitude came together, and were confounded, because that every man heard them speak in his own language. And they were all amazed and marvelled, saying one to another,

Behold, are not all these which speak Galilaeans? And how hear we every man in our own tongue, wherein we were born? Parthians, and Medes, and Elamites, and the dwellers in Mesopotamia, and in Judaea, and Cappadocia, in Pontus, and Asia, Phrygia, and Pamphylia, in Egypt, and in the parts of Libya about Cyrene, and strangers of Rome, Jews and proselytes, Cretes and Arabians, we do hear them speak in our tongues the wonderful works of God.
Acts 2:1-11

On the day of Pentecost, Jews from every race, tribe, and tongue gathered to perform their ritual religion. It was at this moment that God spoke directly to them through the uneducated Jewish fishermen and Jewish women who followed Jesus. Through the work of the Holy Spirit, they would hear their native tongues, and Peter would declare the arrival of their Messiah. God brought them to this place so they would hear His plans and accept Him as Savior. Peter preached to them with the voice of the Holy Spirit. It was here that these few, true Jews resumed the work of taking the Gospel to all nations. In one day, three thousand men and women of Jewish descent, from all around the world, had come, seeking the will of God. That day, they found it. They found their King and were restored to the Living God, the Father who led Abraham into a land of promise. God fulfilled His promise. The true Jews, throughout history, continued in obedience to His plans. God never intended racism. He is above the fallibility of man. His will is being accomplished in every area and He will reap His harvest from around the world.

And he shall set up an ensign for the nations, and shall assemble the outcasts of Israel, and gather together the dispersed of Judah from the four corners of the earth.

Isaiah 11:12

The Jesus Genealogy

Tracing the purpose and intention of God towards humanity has been our goal. I feel that a good foundation has been laid concerning how God investigates the heart of each person. Fragmented people fail to see the necessity of correctly dividing Truth because the fallen nature within man is only concerned with its own perception of truth based on its own distorted and twisted existence. As we participate in the great plan of God, we must always acknowledge a Higher Truth than our own. We must recognize that God's desire for us is part of His plan of restoration in a fallen world. We must seek to fulfill our role in service to His purpose without letting the fight and the struggle with our inadequacies cause us to be in opposition to His plans. Our ability to seek Truth and gain God's wisdom is the advantage given to those who find themselves befuddled as they go through life, confused by an enemy whose highest aspiration is to confound God's plan. The devil's greatest tactic is to incite men to blame one another so he can conquer and divide. We all must recognize that carnal people tend to look externally and therefore only see what external people have done to them. Without internal revelation, we are all blind to the powers which would easily overwhelm us and influence our feelings. When this onslaught succeeds, our beliefs and actions conflict with the purposes and the intent of God.

As we have journeyed together, we have realized that God places people in every nation, with no intention to exclude any peoples. He desires all people to be saved and works to establish righteousness in every nation. When the Jews became a nation and started practicing racism like the other pagan nations, God scattered them across the world so that every nation would become aware of the One True God. Those Jews who desired God would seek Him and find Him, and would study the Holy Word so that, when the Gospel was released to every nation, they would recognize that Jesus was the fulfillment of prophecy.

Even though a seeker finds Jesus to be authentic, this realization is inadequate if he resumes his application of a Jesus that comes only for his specific race. To the Jew, He comes for the Jew, and to the Greek, for the Greek. This short-sighted mindset finds expression in every nationality. Maybe it is because we recognize that we, personally, need a Savior. We also recognize that our family needs a Savior, our neighbors, our community, and on and on and on. The problem is, we do not see the big picture. Humans tend to be short-

94

sighted because we perceive only those things which we know in our surroundings. Most of us are surrounded by people of our own nationality, or family relations that look like us. This limitation inadvertently hinders our belief concerning how far our God can reach. Satan plays on these limitations, prompting us to engage in, "my God, your God" scenarios. Our teaching, motivation, and understanding restrict our knowledge of God to the confines of our own communities' beliefs. Our refusal to turn from and surpass culture and tradition skews our understanding of God's Word and limits our growth in His purpose.

As I endeavored to obey God concerning this study, He directed me to look online at the pictorial representations of Jesus. As I searched, I found all sorts of pictures representing our Savior. There are pictures of Jesus composed by artists reflecting every nationality from Anglo to African, and from Eskimo to Alien. While this is a testimony of how personally we need and see Jesus, we must be careful not to make a Jesus that is exclusively accessible to our nationality. We must aspire to follow His Word and not make omissions for people groups based on our struggles.

Simply put, all people face struggles when pursuing God. There are personal issues that arise in every aspect of life and people must acknowledge and apply the Truth of God's Word to overcome them. The problem is that we assume there is a place that humanity can reach where this struggle stops. I tell you the truth, there is. It is called heaven and we are not there yet. All people, of all nationalities, face the struggle of the human condition. We fail to respond and act right in the face of complicated circumstances. Various groups, whether racial, social, religious, or political seem to find themselves believing the lie that somewhere outside their current existence is a group of individuals living where struggle does not exist. No matter the skin or condition you are in, you will always carry the human you with you. To change existences, you must know the presence of God through the work of the Holy Spirit and the wisdom of the Word. Then your life must be Spirit-led, nurturing a deep love for God that perpetuates the desire to obey. In the moments you successfully achieve God's goal, you must acknowledge that, during the process of growth, you simply learned to be taught and corrected. For those serving God out of selfish motivation, correction tends to be a problem for the uncrucified sin nature, since it wants to live its own way. It wants to change God, use the victim tactic, access the blame game, twist a verse of text for personal use, or choose to avoid the light of God altogether.

The pursuit of God fails if I take Jesus and attempt to make Him in my image. It is the contrary, seeking and desiring to conform increasingly to His image. Religion uses aspects of God and manipulates them into personal images that appeal to the people they serve. The greatest aspiration for God's people is to be transformed into His image so that we live to please the God we serve. In so many ways, we continue to place God in our plans instead of placing our plans in His hands. While there is nothing wrong with images or ideas that make Jesus relatable to us as our Savior, we must always realize that Jesus is not exclusive to our racial depiction. To make such a claim makes us idolaters and limits God to an image we have made.

Thou shalt not make unto thee any graven image, or any likeness [of any thing] that [is] in heaven above, or that [is] in the earth beneath, or that [is] in the water under the earth.
Exodus 20:4

Is it possible that our version of Jesus is merely another graven image? Do we find ourselves carving up Scripture to make sure God meets the criteria that make people most comfortable? By excluding parts of Scripture and rejecting aspects of the Word, we become the creators of our own religious demise. These types of mindsets pervert the purpose of God toward all people within His creation. As I study the Word, I find that there are parts of the texts with which I have difficulty. Yet I dare not seek to change them in my limited understanding. I would rather hold onto them and cherish them until the time comes that I gain an understanding of their application in my life. Carnality just screams out, "Well that is not for me!" Who am I to oppose what God is trying to give to me? Who am I to stand in opposition to what He knows I need? Our segmented societies and personal prejudices recreate God according to our comfort. This is extremely dangerous.

As we seek to trace the genealogy of Jesus, let us understand that nationality had nothing to do with His divinity. The state of humanity did. Scripture is the source that gives us even deeper clues to Jesus' *natural* identity. In the end, all races, through sin and demonic forces, ended up destroying His natural visage as He laid down His life to restore mankind's inner relationship.

Behold, my servant shall deal prudently, he shall be exalted and extolled, and be very high. As many were astonied at thee; his visage was so marred more than any man, and his form more than the sons of men: So shall he sprinkle many nations; the kings shall shut their mouths at him: for that which had not been told them shall they see; and that which they had not heard shall they consider.
Isaiah 52:13-15

For he shall grow up before him as a tender plant, and as a root out of a dry ground: he hath no form nor comeliness; and when we shall see him, [there is] no beauty that we should desire him. He is despised and rejected of men; a man of sorrows, and acquainted with grief: and we hid as it were [our] faces from him; he was despised, and we esteemed him not.
Isaiah 53:2-3

As far as image is concerned, God needed to fulfill His promise to Abraham, but the distorted view taken by humanity concerning the nationality and race of Jesus attempts to stop the very reason God took a body in the first place. The external image was not held as a standard to be worshipped. The true image of humanity and sin was revealed as the outward man was destroyed so the inward man would be restored and glorified to resurrection. All the beauty, or comeliness of mere humanness was marred externally so that earthly image would not be worshipped. God knew that nationality and religion sought to make a god in their own image. He also knew the vanity of man. He knew that the pomp of the crowd would seek to glorify the external man. The external man was what needed to die because of the sin nature within it. This is why He paid the price so that all people who desired Him would be sprinkled with His blood and cleansed from all unrighteousness. The resurrected body of Christ still has in it the evidence of the piercing and the damage of the scars so that we would know he identified with our pain, but once He ascended his image goes far beyond the state of any natural man.

And in the midst of the seven candlesticks [one] like unto the Son of man, clothed with a garment down to the foot, and girt about the paps with a golden girdle. His head and [his] hairs [were] white like wool, as white as snow; and his eyes [were] as a flame of fire; And his feet like unto fine brass, as if they burned in a furnace; and his voice as the sound of many waters.
Revelation 1:13-15

In the end, we are the ones that need to be transformed. Yet, we continue in our human divisions. While this is expected of the world, it should not be practiced in the Church of the living God. We must

100

acknowledge these truths and understand the breakdown of the body of Christ as we take on worldly perspectives. When God put on flesh He put on the flesh of every man, yet humanity continues to practice separation. We make an image of Jesus that is appealing to us when we should be appealing to God. Jesus touched man in every point of life. He was born in a stable yet was paraded in the streets. He spoke doctrine with the highly educated and presented parables to the common man. He healed the sick and accepted one of his disciples as a physician. He touched many races, and the races of the nations were touched by Him. Our spirit was created to take on the character and qualities of God. We were supposed to represent God on the earth and obey Him as His messengers and ambassadors. Instead, men love darkness more than light and fail to resist the influence of the sin man. The first Adam is always carnal yielding to the natural pleasures in the earth, but Jesus came as the second Adam to pay for sins separation and to restore man's union to God. God put on flesh to bring victory instead of leaving us in defeat.

Who, being in the form of God, thought it not robbery to be equal with God: But made himself of no reputation, and took upon him the form of a servant,

and was made in the likeness of men: And being found in fashion as a man (human being), he humbled himself, and became obedient unto death, even the death of the cross.
Philippians 2:6-8

For we have not an high priest which cannot be touched with the feeling of our infirmities; but was in all points tempted like as [we are, yet] without sin.
Hebrews 4:15

For this [is] good and acceptable in the sight of God our Saviour; Who will have all men to be saved, and to come unto the knowledge of the truth. For [there is] one God, and one mediator between God and men, the man Christ Jesus.
1 Timothy 2:3-5

In the Word of God, we find that Jesus did not die for a few, but for all. He is God, and there is no race of fallen humanity that He intended to reject. If rejection happens it is our doing and not His.

In the context of race and ancestry, we find two different genealogies for Jesus. Luke's account represents the perfecting of man's blood and takes us back to Adam. This genealogy brings us to the second Adam being born of a virgin declaring that this is no ordinary man, but rather that Jesus is begotten of God.

This is considered the royal line of Jesus which reaffirms that Jesus is the restorer of the sons of God. The second genealogy is in Matthew and originates with Abraham, thus setting the stage for men to walk by faith to fulfill God's plan. It establishes that God uses broken people to accomplish His will as they yield to His Spirit and desire a relationship with Him. This lineage is especially important to understand because this lineage opens God's love for all races and all humanity. Instead of tracing backward to prove a connection of blood, it starts from Abraham and moves forward so the reader can see God desiring to work with mankind through the work of faith that leads to the blood of Jesus.

The book of the generation of Jesus Christ, the son of David, the son of Abraham. Abraham begat Isaac; and Isaac begat Jacob; and Jacob begat Judas and his brethren; And Judas begat Phares and Zara of Thamar; and Phares begat Esrom; and Esrom begat Aram; And Aram begat Aminadab; and Aminadab begat Naasson; and Naasson begat Salmon; And Salmon begat Booz of Rachab; and Booz begat Obed of Ruth; and Obed begat Jesse; And Jesse begat David the king; and David the king begat Solomon of her [that had been the wife] of Urias; And Solomon begat Roboam; and Roboam begat Abia; and Abia begat Asa; And Asa begat Josaphat; and Josaphat begat Joram; and Joram begat Ozias; And Ozias begat Joatham; and Joatham

*begat Achaz; and Achaz begat Ezekias; And Ezekias
begat Manasses; and Manasses begat Amon; and
Amon begat Josias; And Josias begat Jechonias and
his brethren, about the time they were carried away to
Babylon: And after they were brought to Babylon,
Jechonias begat Salathiel; and Salathiel begat
Zorobabel; And Zorobabel begat Abiud; and Abiud
begat Eliakim; and Eliakim begat Azor; And Azor
begat Sadoc; and Sadoc begat Achim; and Achim begat
Eliud; And Eliud begat Eleazar; and Eleazar begat
Matthan; and Matthan begat Jacob; And Jacob begat
Joseph the husband of Mary, of whom was born Jesus,
who is called Christ.*
Matthew 1:1-16

While the Luke genealogy follows the Jewish
tradition for genealogy by naming the begats through
men that led back to royal sonship, it is restorative of
man because it deals with the prophecy of Satan being
crushed by the seed of a woman. This account points us
back to God being the Father that indwelled Jesus. His
rulership brought forth Jesus as King and ruler of all,
since His Spirit ruled over the sin nature bringing the
defeat of every enemy.

The genealogy listed in the text of Matthew contains
both men and women who followed God by being led by
the Spirit. It confronts the idea of ancestry and natural
race by the fact that the line has many races grafted in

through the obedience of women. In the Old Testament, and human culture, the race of the child was determined by the natural father, and this became their racial identity on the earth. When dealing with the genealogy listed in Matthew, the idea of racial identity loses its power as men and women follow the Spirit of God. This overcomes racial limitations and carnal nature. It allows humanity to become participants in God's plans, regardless of race. In the face of racial and gender issues, God reveals four women in the Matthew genealogy that would be used to achieve His plans. The first female that is mentioned in this genealogy is Tamar.

And Judah begat Pharez and Zarah through Tamar
Matthew 1:3

Tamar was not a daughter born in the lineage of Abraham. Her race was Palestinian, and she was a Canaanite. Judah had previously taken a wife and produced three sons. The first was by the name of Er, the second Onan, and the third was Shelah. When Judah found Tamar, he presented her in marriage to his first son Er. Er was very wicked in God's sight so he died. According to Jewish custom Onan should take his brother's place with his widow to produce an heir for Er.

For some reason, Onan did not want to produce a child with Tamar, yet acted like he would. Some scholars believe that it was because it would compete with his own lineage. Others think he had a racial problem with Tamar being a Canaanite. Either way, he displeased the Lord and he died also. Judah told Tamar that he would give her to his third son, Shelah when he came of age. Instead, he did not give her to his other son and time seemed to pass her by. God had placed a deep desire in Tamar that she would produce an heir. In her despair, she pretended to be a harlot to trap Judah, and Judah lay with her, and she became pregnant. God set up the scenario and exposed Judah's mistakes in the process. Judah did not run from his mistakes but instead acknowledged his failures.

And Judah acknowledged [them], and said, She hath been more righteous than I; because that I gave her not to Shelah my son. And he knew her again no more. And it came to pass in the time of her travail, that, behold, twins [were] in her womb.
Genesis 38:26-27

God always knows what he is doing. It was in his purpose that Tamar the Palestinian would bring forth the heir in the lineage of Christ. While the methods Tamar

used were deceptive and manipulative, her twins would
be used to declare the future purpose of Christ.

*And it came to pass in the time of her travail, that,
behold, twins [were] in her womb. And it came to pass,
when she travailed, that [the one] put out [his] hand:
and the midwife took and bound upon his hand a
scarlet thread, saying, This came out first. And it came
to pass, as he drew back his hand, that, behold, his
brother came out: and she said, How hast thou broken
forth? [this] breach [be] upon thee: therefore his name
was called Pharez. And afterward came out his brother,
that had the scarlet thread upon his hand: and his
name was called Zarah.*
Genesis 38:26-30

During the birthing process, the child that the
midwife thought would be born first ended up later in
succession. The first to be born was named Pharez which
means, "the wall is broken down." This phrase correlates
to a New Testament text that declares a breaking down
of a wall between Jew and Gentile.

*For he is our peace, who hath made both one, and
hath broken down the middle wall of partition between
us; Having abolished in his flesh the enmity, even the
law of commandments contained in ordinances; for to*

make in himself of twain one new man, so making
peace.
Ephesians 2:14-15

While all the human efforts in the Old Testament fall short of God's perfection, He still used people in His providence. Though Tamar deceptively did things, God planned to have her in His line. Pharez's entrance made a powerful statement. But the second son would supersede the first by far.

When the second son reached out first, there was a scarlet thread placed on His hand. When he came forth, he was called Zarah, whose name means, "the light is rising." While God reached out to men in the Old Testament, He would bring light to them in the New. The order of the second son is prophetic concerning the second Adam. The thread in the child's hand signifies that the blood of Jesus would purify the line of men. They would not be purified through any racial or legal means but through a line of blood. God made plans to purify men Himself.

We have also a more sure word of prophecy;
whereunto ye do well that ye take heed, as unto a

light that shineth in a dark place, until the day dawn,
and the day star arise in your hearts.
2 Peter 1:19

Men want to divide race by blood. But Jesus is the true purifier of man's blood, and He is the light that came into the world to light all men. No matter a person's race or background, if they hold onto the bloodline of Christ, God will lead them.

And Salmon begat Boaz through Rahab
Matthew 1:5

Born in a distant land and associated with the culture of moon worshipping idolatry and false gods of fertility, God found a woman named Rahab. Her story is one of impurity and harlotry. Her nationality is Arab, and her people were the nation of the Canaanites. The plain fact that she was a Canaanite should have condemned her, but God had another plan. Her name means "a growing liberty makes room for you."

The time had come for the people of God to confront the racism and idolatry of Jericho. Spies were sent out to investigate the city. It seemed that they would be discovered. But instead of turning God's men over to the pagan government, Rahab hides and protects

God's people within her house. Her participation
revealed a willingness to let go of her own culture and
heritage to lay hold of the bloodline of Christ.

*Behold, [when] we come into the land, thou shalt bind
this line of scarlet thread in the window which thou
didst let us down by: and thou shalt bring thy father,
and thy mother, and thy brethren, and all thy father's
household, home unto thee.*
Joshua 2:18

*And the young men that were spies went in, and
brought out Rahab, and her father, and her mother,
and her brethren, and all that she had; and they
brought out all her kindred, and left them without the
camp of Israel.*
Joshua 6:23

By faith, Rahab was grafted into the line of Abraham
by believing in the God of Israel and choosing to bind
God's blood to her house. Culture could not hold her or
her family. As the city was destroyed around them, they
were joined to the people of God and became part of
God's family on the earth. Her son would be Boaz, and
his name means "God will perform His work quickly."
When we let go of the world systems, transformation
occurs, and we find God changing the family through new

birth and regeneration. While Boaz would learn God's ways and be identified as a Jew, his relationship with God had nothing to do with nationality. He would be known as a kinsmen redeemer to a woman who was identified as a Gentile by race.

... and Boaz begat Obed through Ruth
Matthew 1:5

Not only does God reach out to every race, tribe, and tongue, but He also reaches out to people who are of mixed race. Ruth was born of many races. In her day, this caused a severe cultural crisis. Because of her multicultural heritage, she would be denied entrance into any group. She would be considered, not-quite-enough of any race to be recognized and accepted. Her skin would not be the right color. Her features would not match any existing pure racial group. She was a Moabite, and the people of Moab were so mixed that their name means, "from father, what father?" The name Ruth means, "friendship," and she was dedicated to her mother-in-law, Naomi, after Ruth's Jewish husband had died. Not only was she dedicated to Naomi, but, deep down, she had rejected all her cultural conflicts and completely embraced the One true God.

And Ruth said, Intreat me not to leave thee, [or] to return from following after thee: for whither thou goest, I will go; and where thou lodgest, I will lodge: thy people [shall be] my people, and thy God my God.
Ruth 1:16

Again, according to Jewish custom, the brothers of her deceased husband were to help her produce an heir for him. They wanted her husband's property but, in the end, rejected her because of her nationality. At the last moment, a distant cousin of her husband stepped in to become her kinsman redeemer. Of course, his name is Boaz. God had prepared him for this moment because his mother had been Rahab the Arab Canaanite who was delivered from pagan harlotry. He was anointed for this purpose and preordained to be the one who would pay the price. With this in mind, we need to remember that this genealogy is a foreshadowing of Jesus being the redeemer of all nationalities. On the day that Boaz paid the full price to purchase the land and Ruth, an interesting declaration is made.

And let thy house be like the house of Pharez, whom Tamar bare unto Judah, of the seed which the LORD shall give thee of this young woman. So Boaz took Ruth, and she was his wife: and when he went in unto

her, the LORD gave her conception, and she bare a
son.
Ruth 4:12-13

This prophetic word continues to declare God's
desire to break all racism as it references back to Tamar
and her son Pharez. God is repeating again, that the
walls of racism would be broken down if the light of
Christ would arise in men's hearts and they would lay
hold of the bloodline of Christ.

and Obed begat Jesse; And Jesse begat David the
king; and David the king begat Solomon of her [that
had been the wife] of Urias
Matthew 1:5-6

Out of the marriage of Boaz and Ruth, God brought
forth their son Obed whose name means "a servant who
labors for God." His commitment to God would sow
seeds of relationship which would bear fruit in King
David. David leads us to another gentile relationship in
the genealogy of Jesus; a woman named Bathsheba. In
the genealogical reference, she is listed as being the wife
of a man named Uriah whom David plotted against and
commanded to be murdered. Bathsheba was a Hittite,
and her lineage was from the people of present-day

Turkey. The Hittites were known assassins and terrorists. Bathsheba's name means, daughter of an oath." This shows us that, somewhere down the line, her father, a foreigner, had made an oath to serve King David. Her father's name was Eliam, which means "God is my kin." An oath to David led to an oath to God. Breaking from the Hittite culture, they found themselves in service to God by joining with the nation of Israel. Bathsheba was married to one of David's mighty men named Uriah the Hittite. Uriah means, "Jehovah is my light." Their commitment to David and his God was genuine and unwavering. God desired to bring them into His plans. David saw Bathsheba and something internal must have let him know that Solomon would be born. But instead of depending on God, David was led by his carnal nature and sinned against the Lord by not trusting Him to fulfill His plans, His way. Even through sin and failure, God used David and Bathsheba to fulfill His purpose because David repented and continued to seek His will. Biblically, we know that Bathsheba would give birth to Solomon, who would build God's house. Solomon's name means, "peace," and is the root for the name of God's city, Jerusalem. Jerusalem means, "teaching of peace." While Solomon built the Jewish temple, his love for other cultures would take his peace away. In the end, God would no longer be his first love and he would be overtaken by the pagan cultures that came through an internal lust for many loves.

To investigate the Genealogy of Jesus is to find that God is accomplishing His plans using humanity. Even in our failures, He calls out to us and asks us to join Him in His journey to be a part. Race and nationality are not important. What is important is to learn to be a yielded and pliable vessel. The color of Jesus does not matter. His racial heritage is of little use. What matters is that He was God in the flesh, and that He died for all people of every tribe, race, and tongue. If you want to know what Jesus looks like, you need to know that Jesus appears whenever people are filled with the Spirit of God and long to be used in God's plans.

While this imagery is used to demonstrate the diversity of Jesus to the nations, that same diversity of man is a distinguishing characteristic of the Body of Christ. The Body of Christ is made up of all races and tribes. The physical body and its attributes cannot be the source of our claim in Christ. It is not reserved for a certain lineage, nationality, or family line. It is given to those who come to God and accept new, spiritual birth by being born again. The inward transformation shows outward character and declares that we are a part of the body of Christ. We are all races, all colors, delivered from all backgrounds, and we have walked out of many cultures and worldly associations. It is not enough to have a picture of Jesus or to remember Him as a figure in history. We are His body, and His Spirit resides in temples not made by hands. We are His people and when you see the body of Christ, you see Jesus in *our* skin.

The body of Jesus is not bound within a tomb or in a national cemetery. It is not distinguished by a specific skin color or nationality. The Body of Christ consists of people of all nations. The Body of Christ is seen when the Spirit of the Lord indwells the human temple.

The Jesus Race

The character and beliefs of the people within a nation have always been instrumental in determining the integrity of the nation itself. Using race to determine the character of a people never really reveals the identity of the citizenry that is present. Every individual within a society contributes to that society in some way. Some yield to sin in nature and others to righteousness. While all people find both existences within themselves, the latter choose to fight the nature that steals, kills, and destroys by demanding its submission to the ways of God and conscience. The conscience of man is the rallying cry of the image of God that seeks to do right from within. If most of the citizenry seeks unity of this fashion, then there is a bond that goes far beyond race, class, national pride, wealth, and the cliques that bring society's woes. The unity of these people is found in a greater source, nature's God.

Manmade governments around the world seek to unify a people by demanding conformity. This conformity tends to be a bending of the will to accept the agenda of the greedy and all-powerful state system. To exist in a wicked nation, one must slowly accept the national agenda which forces everyone to step in line. When governments use power to coerce the people, they manipulate compliance to represent strength by numbers. They no longer care about the citizens and their individual rights and consciences. They only care about power, wealth, and the advancement of their agenda so they can hold people in bondage by making them answer to the state as their sole source of survival. To become that source, the government must indoctrinate the populace to accept that government is their source of peace and safety. To achieve this goal, they often promote narratives of disunity so that groups resent and compete with one another as they grovel for the scraps that are thrown from the all-powerful government table.

People find themselves dependent on God and their neighbor for their basic survival when a nation first begins. But, as the nation grows, the sinfulness of men also increases. As people and politician get their eyes on materialism and the acquisition of power, the populace replaces God and turns to the humanistic ideas of man worship. Over time, the idea of nation-building moves away from building individual character to constructing a huge system, like a black hole, absorbing all the power and wealth of the nation. According to world101.cfr.org nation building is "a significant undertaking that governments employ to develop political, economic,

security, and social institutions in other countries—
especially those emerging from conflict." So "nation
building" is solidifying your own nation's power and
influence by capitalizing on the devastation of another
nation. But what if the same methods could be used to
rebuild its nation from within? If a government seeks to
transform righteous people within its nation and bring
them into conformity, it must have constant emerging
conflict and appear to be the savior. This is the mindset
of the humanistic government systems; conquer through
division. When men are governed by lust, division is a
way of life. One must conquer another to acquire more
stuff and we all know a house divided against itself
cannot stand.

While individuals who seek God and righteousness
are unified by the relationship with God from within, the
lust-filled man uses his life for the all-consuming "I."
They hide their shortcomings and selfishness, but let
fame, greed, self-attainment, and jealousy rule and make
choices in their lives. In the end, the word "nation" refers
to a group of people with a common interest, working
together and living their lives towards a unified goal. The
question is "What is the goal and what source is unifying
the people?"

119

Our diversity and resilience are meant to be a valuable tool in our arsenal as a nation. But without God and conscience to defend us, we are consumed by our enemy, lust. We further our sinful collective interests and they become the chief source of anarchy and division amongst ourselves. Like the prodigal son, we have left our Father and have become reckless and full of contempt. Humanity is debilitated with flaws. It takes God to help us recognize our shortcomings and errors.

Currently, our government centers on clashes between officials who focus on rebuilding our nation through division and conflict, and those who work to build the character of God within the people. Because of the motive of division, scattering occurs. This is exactly what happened to the Jewish people as they left God and followed the ways of the other humanistic governments. The greatest threat to a government system that rules by tax revenue and numbers as its primary resource is for people not to comply with the plan.

Officials start to view the people in opposition to their ideologies as a disease that must be eradicated before they infect more of the populace. This idea is pervasive beyond national governments. It is a string of thought that runs through community organizers, religions, capitalist monopolies, racial groups, and all men who seek to consolidate people for a power statement. The greatest fear of carnal, man-made organizations is that they lose people and the control they have over them. This glorification of control finds its root in the sinful nature itself. It is a form of slavery that seeks to subjugate and control humanity. Man goes farther down the path of slavery and destruction when he chooses to make government and leaders his source and blinds himself to the fact that the way to freedom is to return to God. This return is not a form of subjugation, but rather a free choice to love the purposes and plans of God. God does not rule by numbers. Instead, He rules by purpose and sacrificial love. God never loses anyone; He knows where the heart is and simply waits for you to wake up in the pig pen and head back home. As people begin to wake up and turn back to God, corrupt politicians immediately feel threatened. This is exactly the fear expressed by the nation builders of Israel when Jesus arrived on the scene.

Then gathered the chief priests and the Pharisees a council, and said, What do we? for this man doeth many miracles. If we let him thus alone, all [men] will believe on him: and the Romans shall come and take away both our place and nation. And one of them, [named] Caiaphas, being the high priest that same

year, said unto them, Ye know nothing at all, Nor consider that it is expedient for us, that one man should die for the people, and that the whole nation perish not. And this spake he not of himself: but being high priest that year, he prophesied that Jesus should die for that nation; And not for that nation only, but that also he should gather together in one the children of God that were scattered abroad.
John 11:47-52

The fastest way to destroy the plans of weak, inferior, man-made government is for the people within a nation to return to God and seek His righteousness. Every demonic faction will be nullified when the propaganda narrative of division is silenced and the people hear the resounding theme of the nativity. For this to occur, God must be placed where He belongs within every heart.

And suddenly there was with the angel a multitude of the heavenly host praising God, and saying, Glory to God in the highest, and on earth peace, good will toward men.
Luke 2:13-14

And the angel said unto them, Fear not: for, behold, I bring you good tidings of great joy, which shall be to all people.
Luke 2:10

The greatest fear of the antichrist system is that people of every tribe race and tongue will stop seeking government and start seeking Christ. The government is dependent on the compliance of its subjects and, therefore, works to acquire greater power and wealth to exert increasing influence over more people. When people turn to God their agenda is nullified because the people turn to a different source with unlimited power and never-ending wisdom. Not a limited god, but a God that can touch people across national boundaries and racial divisions. This is why the nations seek to destroy Christianity and the personal relationship with Christ.

The Jewish government in Jesus's day hated Him and found the remedy in the goal of His destruction. At one of His teaching sessions, their evil hearts trembled at the thought of His teaching being dispersed among the Gentiles.

Then said Jesus unto them, Yet a little while am I with you, and [then] I go unto him that sent me. Ye shall seek me, and shall not find [me]: and where I am, [thither] ye cannot come. Then said the Jews among themselves, Whither will he go, that we shall not find him? will he go unto the dispersed among the Gentiles, and teach the Gentiles?
John 7:33-35

For those who seek control, nothing is more intimidating than groups of people who no longer need their services to live their lives. It is very threatening to think that your power stops with material infrastructure such as roads and buildings, instead of convincing a populace that you rule their lives. God is not a limited resource, and when man seeks to follow Him, the freedom discovered in the growth process far outweighs the perceived safety other men can give. When people are ruled by God, the government that desires to be all-powerful must settle for submission to God and become the people's servants. This is the correct aspiration of every sphere of government from the pulpit to the palace. But without Christ at the center of the leader, it cannot occur. Having limited reach, the leader seeks to subjugate the people closest to him. It starts in the local government and creeps to the national level. Even after it has obtained prominence, it continues to press for more, never reaching satisfaction.

When elitism starts, the people around you plot their plan because they want to be elite too. Power-hungry politicians wear a smile. But inwardly, they are ravening wolves waiting to devour those in power so they can take their place. Jesus came to earth with no intention to participate in this type of agenda. He came as a bridge to restore people back to God so they would be as free as possible, being loosed from the subjugation of sin. This idea becomes a problem when it does not fit with a lust filled agenda capitalizing on class, race, religion or political systems. God's way of unifying people went across class and racial barriers and unified the followers in the heart through the work of the Holy Spirit. God has no problem with the boundaries of nations because He is much more interested in the people within them experiencing His power and life-giving principles. Satan offered Christ the world. But Christ had no interest in the acquisition of the physical because it was already His. He wanted to restore people to God so that they would fulfill their purpose of living and governing their lives under God. God's rule will not be limited to a religious system of elitism, class, race, or politics. He is looking for "whosoever will" to come to Him to start the walk of restoration.

And Jesus came and spake unto them, saying, All power is given unto me in heaven and in earth. Go ye therefore, and teach all nations, baptizing them in the name of the Father, and of the Son, and of the Holy Ghost: Teaching them to observe all things whatsoever

I have commanded you: and, lo, I am with you alway,
[even] unto the end of the world. Amen.
Matthew 28:18-20

The purpose of Christ is to change every person from within so they can all be blessed and prosperous without. This becomes a threat to those who seek power and control over others. It is so intimidating to the demonic and world-based systems to think that God is going to beat them in acquisition, that they try to stop His plans. They are in opposition because they desire to be god and rule as if they are in control. Even after the coming of Christ and the experience of the day of Pentecost, the Jewish mindset continually felt the threat of losing their chosen status. This is why the gentile question brought such heated contention. While the Jews had experienced persecution at the hands of foreign governments, they failed to realize that the gentile peoples of the world had been subjugated to evil, demonic government systems that ruled by fear and brutality as well. Jesus was the light that would come, not only to the Jew but to all those who would seek after righteousness. As God, He has always desired the restoration of all peoples. Yet, the darkness has caused people to be ignorant of His ways and plans. God recognized that the world's use of the systems of culture and ethos worked to depict God as having accepted the Jew and stabbed all other people groups in the back. When darkness reigns, the pain of the people is usually expressed as anger toward God. God planned that all people would know His true intentions so they could make a choice. In Greek, the word "gentile" takes us back to the word "ethnos," which limits a person to the habits and customs generated by a human family. In Hebrew, the word is "goee" which means that these people have turned their back on God or even betrayed God's intent. The Gospels were written to open every person to the true knowledge of God as Savior and to make people accountable for their own choice. How can anyone who is ignorant make a choice when they are not aware of God's intent? As the early church appeared on the scene, God sent His Gospel out to people of all races, tribes, and tongues, so they would be allowed to respond.

There was a certain man in Caesarea called Cornelius, a centurion of the band called the Italian [band], [A] devout [man], and one that feared God with all his house, which gave much alms to the people, and prayed to God alway. He saw in a vision evidently about the ninth hour of the day an angel of God coming in to him, and saying unto him, Cornelius. And

127

when he looked on him, he was afraid, and said, What is it, Lord? And he said unto him, Thy prayers and thine alms are come up for a memorial before God. And now send men to Joppa, and call for [one] Simon, whose surname is Peter... And he said unto them, Ye know how that it is an unlawful thing for a man that is a Jew to keep company, or come unto one of another nation; but God hath shewed me that I should not call any man common or unclean... Then Peter opened [his] mouth, and said, Of a truth I perceive that God is no respecter of persons: But in every nation he that feareth him, and worketh righteousness, is accepted with him. The word which [God] sent unto the children of Israel, preaching peace by Jesus Christ: (he is Lord of all)... And they of the circumcision which believed were astonished, as many as came with Peter, because that on the Gentiles also was poured out the gift of the Holy Ghost. For they heard them speak with tongues, and magnify God. Then answered Peter, Can any man forbid water, that these should not be baptized, which have received the Holy Ghost as well as we?
Act 10:1-5, 28, 34-36, 45-47

It is by no accident that God sent Jesus into the world during the days of the strength and might of the Roman Empire. The Roman Empire would encompass forty-eight of the nations of the earth. In its time, those who were conquered were incorporated with the local governments to produce systems of caste, slavery, and racial classification. The antichrist system was already at work and Jesus started His opposition to it with a small band of followers who were empowered by His righteousness and His Spirit. In our minds, it seems like it would be a wonderful experience and a welcoming task. But Peter found himself in opposition to the very culture and ethos in society that he had been taught from birth. God tells Peter, in a vision, not to call unclean what God has made clean. We find out that this vision is directly connected to the next mission that God would ask him to take.

God chose a man named Cornelius to be the first gentile to be presented with the Gospel message. This man was not just a citizen of one of the conquered nations. He was a Roman centurion, organized and regimented in the Italian band. As we all know, Rome was, and remains, the center of the existence of the nation of Italy. It is here that the Gospel makes a resounding statement. God was not just going to convert the lower-class citizenry. He shocked the Jews and the world by reaching out to a home that was of the gentile community, the most despised group that the Jews called the most unclean. He was an Italian and involved in the very antichrist system that plunged the known world into man worship and big government bondage. According to

Peter's ethos, this would be a topic of very heated discussion. Yet God required Peter to obey and fulfill His will above his own personal deficiencies and racial feelings. We would like to assume that Cornelius knew nothing of God, yet the Scripture reveals that God speaks to men desiring righteousness in every society. God tells Cornelius to seek out Peter. As Peter obeys, the Gospel is received, and the Holy Spirit is poured out upon Cornelius and his whole house, striking a blow at class and racial divides.

The Roman centurion was transformed as he obeyed God and yielded. But Peter and the Jewish community would face a struggle of equal proportion as God dealt with their wicked, racist ways as well. One of the greatest proclamations in history filled the mouth of Peter when God spoke His will through him and said, "Of a truth, I perceive that God is no respecter of persons: But in every nation he that feareth him, and worketh righteousness, is accepted with him." How can we be sure it was God giving Peter the words to speak? It could not have been the carnal nature of Peter because it is evident that it took time for him to accept the Gentiles. He was still dealing with racism in later texts of Scripture which condemn his actions and motives concerning eating with the gentiles.

The Jewish church in Jerusalem found itself in many racial and religious debates and arguments. God chose to transform a Jew of Jews who not only persecuted Christians but found status in culture through his Roman citizenship. This only goes to show that religious practice does not shield an individual from the evil desire of being honored in the systems of the world. Only a relationship with God has the power to keep a man on point and in focus. Saul had an inward conversion, and it transformed his desires from the inside out. God removed him from Jerusalem and led him to a group of Christians that resided in Antioch. It was here that God continued to break down racial barriers and it was from this church that the carrying of the Gospel to the Gentiles proceeded.

Now there were in the church that was at Antioch certain prophets and teachers; as Barnabas, and Simeon that was called Niger, and Lucius of Cyrene, and Manaen, which had been brought up with Herod the tetrarch, and Saul.
Acts 13:1

In this short verse, God brought together a group of individuals who would represent the purpose and Spirit of Christ. The congregants would be known as Christians. It was here that racial division was broken, and God's purposes continued to be made known. He chose men to gather that were Christian in purpose, but radically different in their appearance and class.

As a man from Cyprus, Barnabas would have been Greek in appearance and his skin tone would have been that of a mixed, medium complexion. His status was one of a wealthy Levite and he would have been recognized as such in the temple of Jerusalem. Yet, he was known as extremely good-natured and left the confines of the Jewish ways. A man named Simeon was a part of the leadership and it states that he was from Niger. He was dark in complexion and God chose him as a scholarly leader who would be a founding member of the early church. Both he and Lucius of Cyrene are of African nationality intentionally, by God's handiwork and design. As a Christian from the nation of Nigeria, God intended this to be listed in His Word so no man could call Christianity a "white man's" religion. Even today, Apostle Paul would be rejected by the world system's racial classification of white. On Paul's journey in Acts 21, his outward appearance is alluded to when he is accused of being an Egyptian who had led people into a religious revolution. When we go to the Word, we need to understand that God uses people and events to intentionally refer to profound concepts. The point of this text is that the outward appearance of Paul led people to believe that he was of a darker race and implies that there are no racial barriers in Christianity. Christians everywhere must acknowledge that God is not choosing people based on race.

The church of Antioch was a founding congregation that helped establish the majority of the early church congregations. While the church of Jerusalem was in great contention and destroying itself from the inside out, Antioch commissioned Paul and Barnabas to proceed with the work of taking the message of Jesus Christ to the world. The greatest work that can be done for Jesus Christ has nothing to do with a certain nationality or race. It has to do with the hearts of individuals yielding to the nature and the will of God. God saw the members of Antioch as a group of people who revealed His Spirit from the inside out. We know this because it is the congregation of this local assembly that first took on the name of Christian. The identity moved from being one that was simply external religious practice to God's identity being revealed from within the heart of every person. This beginning caused relationships with Christ to spread to all peoples without national boundaries or limits. It is hard for the anti-Christ systems of the world to stop creation's God who does His greatest work from within.

Unlimited Descriptions

To embrace the practice of racism is to embrace the structures of a world system that operates in a core philosophy of limitation. These limitations are set and imposed by a self-appointed elite society or ruling class until the populace believes in them. Once a person embraces belief in the permanence of the system, the very act of believing forms a self-regulating bondage or limitation in their thoughts and actions. Racism takes a permanent, biologically physical attribute and assigns certain character traits to it so that the person believes they, or others, are permanently stuck in their life condition, regardless of choices. Racism is inherently and irrationally divisive since those who practice it make fundamental determinations about their, or another's, worth to society based on irrelevant traits of appearance rather than relevant acts based on individual character. We like to think it is done by one group to another, but it takes both groups to believe in the stereotypes that have been pressed upon their existence. The demonic world system has decided that outward appearance determines temperament, morality, disposition, and intellectual ability. It says that our nationality is set and cannot be changed because of our outward appearance and biology. It defines us when we say that our outward biology means we believe these things, live this way, will always be this way, or operate this way. It can be so powerful that even your biological race can be used to reinforce, in you, the very societal code you detest. In the areas where fundamental differences are not common (we all eat, we all wear clothes, etc.), racism points out the insignificant and petty variances in our common necessities as proof that the dissimilarities between races are too vast to bridge and that one race cannot understand another, as though races are living a different human experience and facing insurmountable incongruencies between their perceptions of reality.

This system of deception surpasses national racial lines. It can be found in the very war between the sin nature that tries to define us and corrupt the changes that God desires to make in every human. The sin nature relentlessly defines us by limitation and weakness. It reminds each of us of some area that we repetitively fail to overcome. We perceive these failures as inherent and insoluble weaknesses in our flesh, genetically imprinted in us at the moment of our conception. The demonic systems capitalize on this weakness and taunt us with the fear that there is nothing that can be done to change it. While the word "flesh" speaks of the fallen sin nature, in the Biblical context, you can easily see how someone would like to capitalize on the fear of its permanence, embrace its power, and propagate the idea that outward biology is the cause of someone's negative existence.

As we continue to understand God's desire to have a relationship with all nations, all people, all tribes, and to gather a people for Himself from all the earth, we must understand the purpose of the Biblical terminology used to describe various people or people groups in the Word of God. The written accounts give us the structures of society so that we will know the limitations of the world systems and the racism that is practiced between nations, governments, and peoples. It also reveals to us the various pagan beliefs, ideals, and practices of societies since their formation and existence. In this way, we realize that, without God, people are deceived, and the selfish sin nature is indiscriminate about who is pillaged, murdered, and destroyed while it seeks to gain power and earthly gain.

The sin nature is so unconcerned with the effects of its actions that the resulting devastation causes whole societies to perpetually rebuild or even strengthen systems of bondage, slavery, and pain in a naive attempt to prevent it. This pattern proves that there is demonic influence. This influence works with fallen man to continually reproduce the very thing from which God has come to free us. The world systems instill division, educating us into set beliefs and opinions, even opinions about ourselves. Humanity operates in limitations, and these limitations should drive us to a God with no limits.

The accounts given to us in the Word of God are unlimited. The Word shows us unlimited descriptions of people who were identified in the world's class, race, religious or social systems. This identification is not in the Word to keep them limited. It is there as a reference so that we begin to perceive a God who helps us overcome limitations. These references are meant to be a resource so we can compare the ethos and beliefs of a certain nation or people and understand the areas of belief that opposed the systems of God. The Bible is a beautiful revelation of reality that illuminates the truth about people. People who were born into all sorts of real-world situations, faced individual weakness, and overcame the world systems of class, pagan religion, race, and creed. Never think you know God enough to restrict Him to your own limitations. To allow God to be the source is to overcome the limitations that come with natural existence, whether those limitations come from within or without.

To be born into a society is to be born into a pre-established set of beliefs, values, and stereotypes. The subjection of individuals to various arbitrary rules of a social order predates the first nation. We become aware of the operational systems as we live in them. We either learn to conform to society or we learn to align with God and change society. The greatest change that can happen in your life is to start a relationship with Jesus. He constantly broke the rules of society in the New Testament because He knew that society was breaking God's rules and hindered the intent of God for all people. The world system creates boundaries for people to subjugate them to government and power. Jesus Christ sets men free from the bondage of sin so that everyone fulfills their God-given purpose. Access to this freedom depends on whether each person chooses to be restored to God to learn His ways. This can seem very abnormal since we are trained by sinful society and often overcome by our own sin nature. We face a twofold battle. It is from man without and our faulty beliefs within. Let us start by looking at this text in John.

Then cometh he to a city of Samaria, which is called Sychar, near to the parcel of ground that Jacob gave to his son Joseph. Now Jacob's well was there. Jesus

therefore, being wearied with [his] journey, sat thus on the well: [and] it was about the sixth hour... Then saith the woman of Samaria unto him, How is it that thou, being a Jew, askest drink of me, which am a woman of Samaria? for the Jews have no dealings with the Samaritans... Our fathers worshipped in this mountain; and ye say, that in Jerusalem is the place where men ought to worship.
John 4:5-6, 9, 20

Samaritans were born into a racial class where people were half Jew and half Gentile. They originated from earlier Jews who had merged with the nation of Assyria. The Samaritans believed that they were the authentic Jewish people perfectly keeping the Mosaic law. They held strong beliefs in the Torah, and they had their special copy of the Pentateuch. They refused to worship God in Jerusalem in preference to the belief that true worship occurred on Mount Gerizim, the place where their ancestors resided. This was identified in Deuteronomy as the mountain of blessing. To the Jews, Samaritans were half breeds and they treated them with great disdain.

Not only did the Jews have a problem receiving the Samaritans, but the Samaritans had a severe problem with the Jews. Racism occurs when people continue to perpetuate systems that cause individuals to stay on their side of town or their side of the street. Jesus violated this system by entering the city of Samaria. He compounded His violation when He waited to meet the woman who came to the well. When He spoke to her, the indoctrination of her culture came spewing out of her mouth. All the negativity and all the racism could immediately be identified through her own words. Instead of stopping the conversation, Jesus offered her the living water that would give her true life. The conversation continued when Jesus asked her about her husband. He reveals she has had five and the man she was currently with was not her husband. By doing this he identified that the Samaritans did not keep the law of Moses as perfectly as they would have liked to pretend, especially to those who are Jews. She tried to deflect with a debate over the proper location to worship God. Jesus revealed that true worship is not about a location but rather from within a person, in the spirit, as a willing vessel longs to hear the Truth. Immediately, the woman at the well had an internal transformation through the work of the Holy Spirit. As the woman received the revelation that Jesus was the Christ she ran into the city and many Samaritans were introduced to Jesus and believed.

In another account, we find that the disciples allowed their indoctrination to try to interfere with God's true intent of breaking down the walls and barriers that held the Samaritans in bondage.

And it came to pass, when the time was come that he should be received up, he stedfastly set his face to go to Jerusalem, And sent messengers before his face: and they went, and entered into a village of the Samaritans, to make ready for him. And they did not receive him, because his face was as though he would go to Jerusalem. And when his disciples James and John saw [this], they said, Lord, wilt thou that we command fire to come down from heaven, and consume them, even as Elias did? But he turned, and rebuked them, and said, Ye know not what manner of spirit ye are of. For the Son of man is not come to destroy men's lives, but to save [them]. And they went to another village.
Luke 9:51-56

This Scripture shows us that the true test was for James and John. Jesus intentionally sent them into the city to ready the people for His teachings. Indoctrinated by society the Samaritans did not hear the teaching and rejected Him at the outset purely because He was a Jew that was faced towards Jerusalem. This demonstrates how deeply people can hold onto a thought process. Not only did it stop them from hearing, but it also made them assume the direction someone of another race or social class would take. As the rejection occurred, the hearts of the disciples were exposed when they desired destruction for the Samaritans instead of a heartfelt desire for salvation. Jesus identified this as the influence of a wrong spirit and rebuked them for taking part in it.

While the effects of racism cause dissension and assumption between people groups, one of the greatest areas of damage occurs within the people themselves. When a person lives in a hedonistic society, devoid of God, they adopt the beliefs and perspectives of the society in which they live. When those beliefs settle in the heart, they cause the person to be trapped internally and externally. This bondage is not limited to a single individual. It occurs in the whole of society as people believe the circulated foolishness of people. Though many do not want any part of it, they are still made a part of the outward racial stereotypes. When the belief is firmly held, those who are the subject of racism accuse all those of another race of being racist, and those who are accused of being racist feel forced to prove that they are not. This type of system takes away individuality and fails to allow room for relationships to be built and truth to be known.

This type of test was what the Syrophoenician woman faced when she approached Jesus about her demonically tormented daughter. She was of mixed race, being half Syrian and half Phoenician. The Jews grouped her with the Canaanites, who worshipped false gods. She was probably from a Greek culture as well since the Greek society had taken over her nation. To the Roman and Greek cultures, national identification was of extreme importance since the officials determined your worth based on your origin of birth. As a lower-class citizen of mixed race, she lived a life as an outcast, as you will see in these verses.

Then Jesus went thence, and departed into the coasts of Tyre and Sidon. And, behold, a woman of Canaan came out of the same coasts, and cried unto him, saying, Have mercy on me, O Lord, [thou] Son of David; my daughter is grievously vexed with a devil. But he answered her not a word. And his disciples came and besought him, saying, Send her away; for she crieth after us. But he answered and said, I am not sent but unto the lost sheep of the house of Israel. Then came she and worshipped him, saying, Lord, help me. But he answered and said, It is not meet to take the children's bread, and to cast [it] to dogs. And she said, Truth, Lord: yet the dogs eat of the crumbs which fall from their masters' table. Then Jesus answered and said unto her, O woman, great [is] thy faith: be it unto

thee even as thou wilt. And her daughter was made whole from that very hour.
Matthew 15:21-28

This encounter depicts a woman who was distraught and cried out for Jesus to deliver her daughter from a tormenting spirit. Instead of responding to her outcry, Jesus gave no response at all. As she continued, the disciples became irritated with her and asked Jesus to send her away. At once, Jesus started a process that would reveal the woman's beliefs and even her faith. He first tested her by seeing if she believed that He was only sent to the Jew. He did this by asserting that very statement. Undeterred, she refused to stop her pursuit. Something occurred inside and her methods changed. Instead of the outcry, her heart turned to a state of worship with a sincere, "Lord, help me." This was the moment of decision for her faith. Jesus declared what society had said about her to see if she believed in the limits that had been placed upon her. Her response revealed that she believed that God was above manufactured systems and that He had the power to meet her as well. Jesus declares "O Woman, great is thy faith." Instantly, her daughter is made whole, all because she rejected the beliefs of her society. The unlimited

God went beyond limits and proved that fabricated restrictions do not have the power to stop God from moving in your life.

The idea that God was beyond racial limits is just as difficult for people to accept in the present culture as it was in Jesus's day. When people are taught wrong concepts, it causes an uproar and can even be dangerous. There is another account of a Syrophoenician woman that Jesus references in Scripture to prove to the Jews that God was outside of the boundary of race. When the Jews asked Him to perform the miracles He did in Capernaum (which means, village of comfort), His response to them made them try to kill Him.

And he said, Verily I say unto you, No prophet is accepted in his own country. But I tell you of a truth, many widows were in Israel in the days of Elias, when the heaven was shut up three years and six months, when great famine was throughout all the land; But unto none of them was Elias sent, save unto Sarepta, [a city] of Sidon, unto a woman [that was] a widow. And many lepers were in Israel in the time of Eliseus the prophet; and none of them was cleansed, saving Naaman the Syrian. And all they in the synagogue, when they heard these things, were filled with wrath, And rose up, and thrust him out of the city, and led him unto the brow of the hill whereon their city was

> *built, that they might cast him down headlong. But he*
> *passing through the midst of them went his way.*
> *Luke 4:24-30*

His reply referenced the Old Testament and declared that God did not send Elijah to the widows of Israel, but instead had him visit a Syrophoenician widow and save her during the famine. He continued by saying that God did not send Elisha to the lepers in Israel. Instead, He sent him to Naaman, the Syrian. When the Jews heard these things, the demonic spirit of racism was so strong that they were filled with violent wrath. They threw Jesus out of the city and led him to the top of the hill where they were going to throw Him down headfirst. Apparently, the idea that God could love people of other races was too much for those who held their social status and religion in such high esteem. Their emotional responses failed to impress God or deter His plans. He simply passed through the midst of them.

Christians are always prepared to fulfill God's will beyond the reactions of the people around them. We cannot join the hurt or try to justify sinful people's natural response that leads to violence. Instead, we must be representatives of the will of God in a world where humanity continues to be indoctrinated in demonic, class

and race-based ideologies that can only result in pain.
There is only one way to bring resolve to these issues
and that is a relationship with Jesus that causes us to see
ourselves as citizens of another kingdom. When evil
takes over and we steal, kill, and destroy, we are no
longer among those who seek God's ways on earth. We
have become a people who have taken on the very
nature we oppose, perpetuating the cycle of pain and
anguish.

*Tribulation and anguish, upon every soul of man that
doeth evil, of the Jew first, and also of the Gentile;
But glory, honour, and peace, to every man that
worketh good, to the Jew first, and also to the Gentile*
Romans 2:9-10

*What then? are we better [than they]? No, in no wise:
for we have before proved both Jews and Gentiles,
that they are all under sin.*
Romans 3:9

A relationship with Jesus is necessary to unify a
people that will declare God's righteousness on earth.
Jesus rules and reigns in our life from the inside first. It
is the character of Christ that must be built from within
that will most affect how people will see you from
without. We do not need to practice the manipulations

that have been placed upon us. We need Jesus to set us free. We need His righteousness and character to be the center of our hearts so we can influence the nation to which we have been assigned.

For there is no difference between the Jew and the Greek: for the same Lord over all is rich unto all that call upon him.
Romans 10:12

For the Jews require a sign, and the Greeks seek after wisdom: But we preach Christ crucified, unto the Jews a stumblingblock, and unto the Greeks foolishness; But unto them which are called, both Jews and Greeks, Christ the power of God, and the wisdom of God.
1 Corinthians 1:22-24

There is neither Jew nor Greek, there is neither bond nor free, there is neither male nor female: for ye are all one in Christ Jesus.
Galatians 3:28

World Reconciliation

Recognizing the Biblical pattern of Christ gives us the ability to identify people seeking an inward relationship with Jesus that bears righteous character, a principled life according to God's purposes, and the Spirit of God who empowers us to love God and others. The worldly pattern contrasts with this in people who practice a form of religion, self-gratification, acquisition of things, political exploitation for power, personal gain, or sin-based justification. The worldly pattern divides and conquers. The Biblical pattern unifies in a search for God's purposes in the earth and desire for the best life outcome for all people. Many organizations and people groups have come, through the centuries, in the name of Christ but have outwardly demonstrated wrong methods and motives. People have often done this willfully and viciously. At other times, the culture and ethos had preset, unbiblical beliefs that went unrecognized and uncorrected within groups of fallen humanity. Wrong ideas take root and what seems logical to a trained people ends up bringing destruction and stands in opposition to God's will and purpose as He created it.

These concepts are not only observed in the societies and political spheres of the pagan world. People often find themselves existing within groups that exalt certain ideas to the level of religion. While nature's God desires freedom and good to be lived from within, the natural, fallen nature seems to think that these things are acquired from without. The result is a form of a totalitarian mindset which seeks the acquisition of all. The scope of this acquisition ranges from material, power, and government, all the way down to taking away an individual's right to hold personal ideas and beliefs. Organizations, governments, and religions are not against using class, racial, or social propaganda to achieve their goals by stimulating groups of people to fear and destroy one another. By initiating fear-based thought, these organizations avoid liability by pointing the finger at the actions of a group instead of letting individuals be known by character. The organization mentions some atrocious events to further undergird beliefs about certain people or groups so that society will assist them in the goal of separating and conquering.

In true, Biblical Christianity, the goal is never the acquisition of any external thing because true Christians know that these things belong to God and are to be placed in humanity's hands to achieve His purposes and use. The first aim of Jesus Christ is to change the individual from within so that the person will govern things placed in his hands in a righteous way. God's idea of reconciliation in no way vilifies a people based on nationality or race. It looks at the individual heart and calls people to account for evil thoughts, beliefs, motivations, and actions. God's desire is to unify all nations, tribes, and tongues based on the willingness of their hearts to be a part of His plans. The world's methods use subjugation and tyranny to achieve their goals. They do this by exploiting the sin nature and its weaknesses. They motivate the populace with materialism. They offer them all that the lust nature desires. They profit from it, then blackmail mankind by threatening to expose people for the very thing they sold to them to make money. They divide and conquer and oppose nature's God and His purposes. They rewrite the purpose and pattern of mankind's existence until the need for external control is replaced by an internal acceptance of the warped standard. This idea is totalitarian, and the achievement of it is the manifestation of the evil desire for man to be God. This scenario has been replayed throughout the centuries as demonic influence and thought fills emperors, oligarchs, governments, popes, CEOs, caliphs, Pastors, School Board Presidents, and any other leaders who seek to capitalize on personal lust by the fallen nature of man.

The intention of creation's God was that He would fill the hearts of people and, through relationship, would restore His purposes in the earth. An inward relationship with God would be the source of love in people's life and would teach them to live what He originally created them for. This God-centered development within man would be the internal motivation. Since the fall, every person has fought a battle with sin and the demonic weakness that endeavors to gain victory through personal overthrow. This relationship with God would be the formation of Judaism, and it would be the reformation of the early Christians. The progressive work of civilization would begin in Mesopotamia and would seed the nations of the earth. The advancement of God's kingdom starts with the relationship with God and would be inside the people who desired Him. Both true and false religion spread from east to west as the population of the earth grew and people explored and settled around the world.

Many people speak of Christianity as being the "white man's religion" or a Western religion. By this time, you should see that such a statement is a farce. These types of statements continue the work of racism and separation that give the world systems control over people by motivating people to act on deception. The focus of Christianity was never to get rich or gain

154

material buildings and locations. It was the motive of
God to enter the hearts of people, all peoples.

*Then Philip went down to the city of Samaria, and
preached Christ unto them.*
Acts 8:5

*And straightway he preached Christ in the synagogues,
that he is the Son of God... But Saul increased the
more in strength, and confounded the Jews which
dwelt at Damascus, proving that this is very Christ.*
Acts 9:20, 22

*Through mighty signs and wonders, by the power of
the Spirit of God; so that from Jerusalem (East), and
round about unto Illyricum (Center of Europe West), I
have fully preached the gospel of Christ.*
Romans 15:19

True Christianity does not consider the flesh when
judging a person's character. While the diversity of man's
outward appearance is beautiful in the eye that beholds
God's creation, it fails to reveal the inward that can be
full of vanity and unaesthetic, under demonic influence,
and even monstrous. Christians seek to crucify the sinful
nature and yield to God. The remedy for every man is a
genuine relationship with Jesus Christ. Christ is the Spirit
of God at work on the internal so God can do His work

155

in the external. God calls to all people, and it is our job to receive Him and align our lives with His plans. Each of us has an integral part to play and must be available to reach beyond man-made limitations and boundaries to see others set free.

Wherefore henceforth know we no man after the flesh: yea, though we have known Christ after the flesh, yet now henceforth know we [him] no more. Therefore if any man [be] in Christ, [he is] a new creature: old things are passed away; behold, all things are become new. And all things [are] of God, who hath reconciled us to himself by Jesus Christ, and hath given to us the ministry of reconciliation; To wit, that God was in Christ, reconciling the world unto himself, not imputing their trespasses unto them; and hath committed unto us the word of reconciliation. Now then we are ambassadors for Christ, as though God did beseech [you] by us: we pray [you] in Christ's stead, be ye reconciled to God. For he hath made him [to be] sin for us, who knew no sin; that we might be made the righteousness of God in him.
2 Corinthians 5:16-21

According to the systems of the world, reconciliation is the acceptance of every man-made ethos by a unification of all cultures through false and contrived peace as each one makes up its own truth and pursues its own sinful agendas. It is an effort to appear just and

156

kind. But there is a secret, wolf-like motivation working to destroy those that oppose the fulfillment of the consolidation of power. They put on a face of acceptance to appear righteous to achieve the goal of world-wide recognition and god-like power. This is why the world systems seek to eliminate true Christians who seek to fulfill God's plans. The world is unified in a self-fulfilling nature, organized through the idea of gratifying the lust of the flesh, the lust of the eyes, and the pride of life. It is the unification of brokenness through sin's weakness. True Christianity denies self by loving God and returning to a relationship that restores His original intent. The Kingdom of God empowers each Christian to be an ambassador of reconciliation to the world, appealing to people's consciences as God speaks to their hearts. When humanity is reconciled to God, true freedom occurs and those who try to move man through greed and lust fail in their pursuit of power and gain. The world systems must oppose God's desire because controlling people is part of the agenda. By seeking to displace God, they yield themselves to be controlled by the gods of this world, rebellious spirits that were expelled from heaven. If mankind is controlled by these gods, the only thing that will be created will resemble hell, even though God seeks to save humanity. God calls every nation, tribe, tongue, race, and class in society. He reaches out from a desire for reconciliation. Be reconciled to Christ.

And this gospel of the kingdom shall be preached in all the world for a witness unto all nations; and then shall the end come.
Matthew 24:14

Wherefore remember, that ye [being] in time past Gentiles in the flesh, who are called Uncircumcision by that which is called the Circumcision in the flesh made by hands; That at that time ye were without Christ, being aliens from the commonwealth of Israel, and strangers from the covenants of promise, having no hope, and without God in the world: But now in Christ Jesus ye who sometimes were far off are made nigh by the blood of Christ. For he is our peace, who hath made both one, and hath broken down the middle wall of partition [between us]; Having abolished in his flesh the enmity, [even] the law of commandments [contained] in ordinances; for to make in himself of twain one new man, [so] making peace; And that he might reconcile both unto God in one body by the cross, having slain the enmity thereby: And came and preached peace to you which were afar off, and to them that were nigh. For through him we both have access by one Spirit unto the Father. Now therefore ye are no more strangers and foreigners, but fellowcitizens with the saints, and of the household of God.
Ephesians 2:11-19

To desire Christ is to desire the restoration of the original condition God intended at creation. The sin nature opposes God and wants the conscience silenced and evil called good so that the pursuit of man's lust will remain the consuming focus of life. The internal deception that people suffer blinds them to the truth that the attainment of this focus is not life. It is a drive to death. This is why the world systems will accept any form of science that opposes God as the source. It is compelled to accept and adopt ideas and narratives that, in the end, bring people to destruction. The various systems need broken people to achieve their goals. They inevitably try to replace God with their intellect, money, popularity, or academic prowess at the expense of people who desperately need their happiness restored by a God that comes to make sense of their lives and set them free. While sin seems good for a season, in the end, it leads to destruction and pain. Only a people seeking God experience victory and declare His glorious name as He restores them to His promise. While the promises of God are "yea" and "amen," people face inward struggles as they fight the fight of faith. God willingly assists us in our efforts, through the work of His Holy Spirit.

God is unacceptable to fallen man because His plan requires a personal death to selfishness. To live to the flesh is to hate God. Death to self, destroys the dream of hearing the people chant your name or your product as the secret to success and the mutually fulfilling goal of popularity and wealth. The difference between man and God is, God does not have favorites. He longs for His promises to be manifest in any people who desire His ways. He is not rewarding a group of monetary donors or political backers who are all in it for a piece of the earthly pie. God has promises attached to every purpose. He knows every person individually. He knows the love or competing affections of each human intimately and His number one goal is to show people their choice about who they really are at the center of their being.

When I therefore was thus minded, did I use lightness? or the things that I purpose, do I purpose according to the flesh, that with me there should be yea yea, and nay nay? But [as] God [is] true, our word toward you was not yea and nay. For the Son of God, Jesus Christ, who was preached among you by us, [even] by me and Silvanus and Timotheus, was not yea and nay, but in him was yea. For all the promises of God in him [are] yea, and in him Amen, unto the glory of God by us. Now he which stablisheth us with you in Christ, and hath anointed us, [is] God; Who hath also sealed us, and given the earnest of the Spirit in our hearts.
2 Corinthians 1:17-22

The most gratifying life is one that is fulfilled from within. God's peace occurs when we do what is right in God's eyes with a love of God as our heart's motive. When we fail to meet the mark and fall into sin, our remedy is to acknowledge our wrong before God and others, receive forgiveness, and realize that tomorrow starts a new day. As Christians, we do not seek to change God's Words. We learn to ask Him for more of His power to live them. The sin nature is crucified through acknowledgment and repentance. Human relationships are restored when we repent and forgive one another, and the promises are revealed as we allow our relationship with Christ to grow as we reach towards His image and likeness. There are no bystanders in this life. Each of us will inevitably be a part of the world system or the Kingdom of God, and each of us will depend on one of these entities. The first longs to subjugate. The second longs to free us from sin and failure and rejuvenate our existence.

And I saw another angel fly in the midst of heaven, having the everlasting gospel to preach unto them that dwell on the earth, and to every nation, and kindred, and tongue, and people, Saying with a loud voice, Fear God, and give glory to him; for the hour of his judgment is come: and worship him that made heaven,

and earth, and the sea, and the fountains of waters. And there followed another angel, saying, Babylon is fallen, is fallen, that great city, because she made all nations drink of the wine of the wrath of her fornication.
Revelation 14:6-8

This book has addressed man's efforts to know one another through outward flesh. History recounts many people of Godly character and righteous behavior who were destroyed as wicked men taught others to make assumptions about groups based on outward appearance. You will find, if you listen in our day, wicked people who continue to promote class and racial propaganda that paint one group of a certain race as good and others as evil. Evil leadership that promotes this rhetoric proliferates class warfare. Overgeneralizations train people to make assumptions concerning someone by examining the flesh. As we are taught, and as belief is activated through world system classifications, we become participants in this nonsense by failing to know individuals one at a time.

A relationship is the key to knowing someone. A selfish man can only learn real and lasting relationships through encounters of regeneration by a relationship with God. People are quick to assert the importance of their existence and experience but become hypocrites when they refuse to value the existence and importance of the people and God with whom they have a relationship. Statements of ethos, culture, race, class, nationality, sexuality, or religion are promoted as people seek personal validation. But none of these prove who we really are or express the true battle that goes on within. The superficial identification systems of the world intentionally keep people ignorant because the sinful nature thrives in darkness and hates anything that requires us to bring our wickedness to the light.

Christianity is relational. It exists in an inner relationship with God that affects our outward relationship with man and requires repentance and confession when we are wrong and forgiveness from the ones we violate. Forgiveness alone does not necessarily alleviate the consequences that come from our actions. Without consequence, we will not grow and learn from our mistakes. The world system has taught people to never admit guilt, especially since it might cost someone money. Pride seeks to escape humiliation, stay in power, and protect monetary interests. This mindset is the reason for the multitudes of lawyers in our day. This is why those in cooperation with the world system love to have the power to circumvent or change laws. It is why

our leaders seek positions of power, so they are immune
from accountability. To be Christian is to know that man
cannot change God's laws and that all people will give an
account. This is why living for Christ, growing in Christ,
and making life decisions for Christ, is everything. The
more a person develops a relationship with Jesus
internally, the more value is placed on the principles that
are discovered in God's Word. Building a relationship
with Jesus starts in the inner man and it is of utmost
importance.

The fallen nature establishes ethos and cultures to
coerce people to follow a tyrannical world system. Those
who follow God and His plans are unified through the
love of God and His ways. It is through acknowledgment
and love for God's principles that true reconciliation
happens between people. In God's plan, people are made
equal according to their acknowledgment of their
weakness and sin. This is how we realize that God's love
desires man to repent, be forgiven, and learn God's ways.
Only then can we genuinely love others as they seek to
live God's principles on earth. There are only two groups
of people that exist. There are those who seek and follow
the sinful nature, and there are those who seek to be
reconciled to God to take on His nature. It is through
our relationships that God reveals the truth about our

164

issues. Our love for God drives us to seek His ways and change how we behave toward others.

The systems of the world also desire to bring change. But the change they offer always finds itself connected to a specific group's benefit. Be sure that a man's agenda might benefit someone, but it always fails in its offering to benefit everyone. Impartiality is understood when we recognize that Jesus died for all people so everyone could have access to the life-giving principles of God. These principles alone have the power to bring the ultimate amount of good to people residing in a fallen world.

For it pleased [the Father] that in him should all fulness dwell; And, having made peace through the blood of his cross, by him to reconcile all things unto himself; by him, [I say], whether [they be] things in earth, or things in heaven. And you, that were sometime alienated and enemies in [your] mind by wicked works, yet now hath he reconciled In the body of his flesh through death, to present you holy and unblameable and unreproveable in his sight Colossians 1:19-22

The Inner Man

Real growth occurs when we are in a relationship with a body of people who reflect Christ. The Body of Christ is those who desire Christ and long to respond correctly to what the Word of God asks of us. While it is not comfortable to the flesh to acknowledge when we miss the mark, it is beneficial to each of us as we seek to fulfill God's plans and acknowledge personal weaknesses. It is in our weakness that God is made strong, and He alone gets all the glory. To operate with Jesus in your skin, a person must recognize weakness, move past the selfishness of the mind, will, and emotions, and allow God to rule the spirit. The spirit is the center of our being, and it is what allows us to have a true relationship with God. The soul is the mind, the will, and the emotions that drive our actions and cause us to make wise or stupid decisions. Our lives influence one another. The question is, what nature are we living in? Is the outward nature our existence or are we seeking God's will inwardly?

To live the outward is to seek outward things. If this is our goal, the carnal selfish nature will war for external things and seek only to please itself at the expense of others. Those who are driven by this motive continue to shut down the Truth of God's Word because it is given to us so that our evil motives will be made plain, and a new life will begin that seeks God in all His glory. We will find that telling people we are a certain race means nothing when we stand before God's throne. Race is useless in identifying whether a person's character is good or bad. Declarations of rich or poor, bus driver or metal worker, might speak some status, but fail to tell me who you are. Even a person's profession of a certain religion fails to indicate their character because the best it can do is tell me the person you are trying to be like or the beliefs to which you aspire, instead of the quality of your character. Labeling yourself as Christian fails to prove the value of your actions and beliefs because denominations have watered down the meaning of the term, and men have taught that God's grace nullifies the need to change or seek His ways. All the rhetoric in the world fails to identify who you really are. Relationship reveals who you are because who we are emanates from within.

For from within, out of the heart of men, proceed evil thoughts, adulteries, fornications, murders,... All these evil things come from within, and defile the man.
Mark 7:21, 23

Blind Pharisee, first cleanse the inside of the cup and dish, that the outside of them may be clean also.
Matthew 23:26 NKJV

Behold, thou desirest truth in the inward parts: and in the hidden [part] thou shalt make me to know wisdom. Purge me with hyssop, and I shall be clean: wash me, and I shall be whiter than snow.
Psalm 51:6-7

The heart is where the transformation must occur to be able to demonstrate to the world the outward manifestation of a transformed life. While people see it externally, the work of God is accomplished internally as we allow Him to speak to us about our own issues. The Word and the Spirit do not speak to destroy us. They wake us up to what God desires to change in us. The deceptive nature of offense constantly reminds us of what others have done to us as we endure the sin nature of others in this fallen world, while it blinds us to the endurance others have shown toward us in our offensive ways. This is the basis of so many of the organizations of people who are associated by their deep sense of personal injury which seek external justice through a sense of retribution. While the cause may seem just, the very people screaming about their pain have caused pain to many others in other ways – sometimes even in precisely the same ways. The power of God is the power to forgive and love others beyond the pain they cause. But this power is not given to us internally without our acknowledgment of the pain we have caused to God and others as well. This recognition is the first step toward His forgiveness and instruction for our lives. This is where the supernatural love of God surpasses all boundaries, and it is here that we willingly seek His correction so that we can be used for His greater purpose.

It is the spirit that quickeneth; the flesh profiteth nothing: the words that I speak unto you, [they] are spirit, and [they] are life.
John 6:63

For he is not a Jew, which is one outwardly; neither [is that] circumcision, which is outward in the flesh: But he [is] a Jew, which is one inwardly; and circumcision [is that] of the heart, in the spirit, [and] not in the letter; whose praise [is] not of men, but of God.
Romans 2:28-29

Do ye look on things after the outward appearance? If any man trust to himself that he is Christ's, let him of himself think this again, that, as he [is] Christ's, even so [are] we Christ's.
2 Corinthians 10:7

Internal character is not developed by seeking things that are outward. It is found by seeking a relationship with Jesus Christ from within. This inward work is a relationship that allows God to transform us into a people of character that represent who God really is. While none of us perform it perfectly, we allow God to call us to account in the areas that require growth. The church has operated for centuries with the world system by instantly declaring that someone is a Christian based on a simple public declaration. A verbal declaration is exciting and necessary, but it takes time to reveal the relational desire of the heart. This has produced millions of people who proudly wear the badge of Christian without a meaningful relationship with Christ which is proven by the deep desire for God to correct our character flaws and help us heal the damage we have caused to others. This is why to live His Word is to love to obey His commands.

Which in other ages was not made known unto the sons of men, as it is now revealed unto his holy apostles and prophets by the Spirit; That the Gentiles should be fellowheirs, and of the same body, and partakers of his promise in Christ by the gospel: Whereof I was made a minister, according to the gift of the grace of God given unto me by the effectual working of his power. Unto me, who am less than the least of all saints, is this grace given, that I should preach among the Gentiles the unsearchable riches of Christ; And to make all [men] see what [is] the fellowship of the mystery, which from the beginning of the world hath been hid in God, who created all things

by Jesus Christ: To the intent that now unto the principalities and powers in heavenly [places] might be known by the church the manifold wisdom of God,... That he would grant you, according to the riches of his glory, to be strengthened with might by his Spirit in the inner man.
Ephesians 3:5-10, 16

For I delight in the law of God after the inward man
Romans 7:22

Jesus, in *your* skin, is the only answer that God has given us to heal the damage done by the sinful failures of all humanity. In all our humanistic efforts to demand justice of others, we fail to see that our own human existence, devoid of Christ, violates our own life as well as the life of others. This realization crosses every boundary, every race, every world system, and it will continue until God is the reason for our existence in every arena. It is easy for humans to see what others have done to them. But what they fail to see is what they have done to others. This is a form of blindness that is only remedied when we sincerely allow God to evaluate our lives and our decisions. This internal relationship teaches us how to be like Him, and bears witness to what God truly desires for each life. But, at the same time, we must admit that our efforts are inadequate in so many areas because other lusts interfere with God's plans.

172

While God can move upon the heart of humanity, it is humanity that must execute His plans and obey His will to see His promises come to pass. This is why we are spiritual and natural beings. It is why God's people are called the body of Christ.

Our identity is not determined by race but by our desire for God's righteousness. If you desire right, then it must start with you allowing Jesus to live through you from an internal relationship. You will find that He saves you from your mistakes and teaches you a way of living centered on a heart of obedience to His will. No matter your race, tribe, your tongue, no matter the social, political, cultural, or ethnic classifications the world has pressured you to live, a relationship with Jesus Christ is a relationship of freedom from all these external demands. It releases you to build a love relationship with God that is one of freedom, healing, growth, faith, empowerment, and joy. We receive access to all the promises that God gives when we allow Jesus to forgive us. It is then that we learn to seek His ways so others can learn of Him and see His results in a broken world that tends to live to the outward existence alone. To be a Christian is more than a prayer. It is more than material benefits. It is a heart desire that seeks God for restoration in every area of life. It is pursuing Jesus even in moments of failure, knowing that He loves us and desires to walk with us until we are taught. We cannot trust ourselves because our condition is one of weakness that leads us to believe things that are not true and bring only negative results. The desire of all peoples should be a deep desire to have "Jesus in your skin." If this is your desire, please read and consider the following prayer. Once you consider it, open your heart, and ask Jesus to come in and rebuild your life through a never-ending relationship of growth and mutual love.

Jesus, I come to you today, laying aside all the teachings of the world and the false beliefs that I have learned. I come to you desiring a sincere relationship with you. I ask you to forgive me because I know you are Lord over all areas, and I ask that you would be Lord of my life. I ask you to heal my pain and the woundedness that I have incurred as I have participated with the beliefs and practices of the world. I choose to crucify my selfish and sinful nature so I can receive Your loving and holy nature. Help me give my actions, thoughts, and life decisions to you. I know that you will save me from yesterday, empower me today and preserve me tomorrow, as I continue in my relationship with you. I find my identity and purpose in you and will not look to the world to identify me. Thank you for creating me and making my life a picture of your individuality as I allow my outward man to demonstrate your love and life principles. I welcome you into my life to use my existence,

In Jesus' Name,
Amen.

To whom God would make known to you what [is] the riches of the glory of this mystery among the Gentiles; which is Christ in you, the hope of glory: Whom we preach, warning every man, and teaching every man in all wisdom; that we may present every man perfect in Christ Jesus.
Colossians 1:27-28

175

References

"Biblical Tables, Nations, and Genealogies"
https://answersingenesis.org/racism/what-about-extra-biblical-tables-nations-genealogies-that-go-back-noah/

"What do we mean by Race, Ethnicity and Diversity?"
https://tilford.k-state.edu/resources/educational-benefits-of-diversity/whatisdiverse.html

"Finding Ham, Shem, and Japheth via Y-Chromosome DNA."
https://jamese.jecrois.org/?p=445

"On the Origin of Human Mitochondrial DNA Differences, New Generation Time Data Both Suggest a Unified Young-Earth Creation Model and Challenge the Evolutionary Out-of-Africa Model"
https://answersresearchjournal.org/origin-human-mitochondrial-dna-differences/

"DNA Trends Confirm Noah's Family"
https://www.icr.org/article/dna-trends-confirm-noahs-family

"Among Many Peoples, Little Genomic Variety"
https://www.washingtonpost.com/wp-dyn/content/article/2009/06/21/AR2009062101726.html

"What's the difference between race and ethnicity?"
https://www.livescience.com/difference-between-race-ethnicity.html

References

"Historical Race Concepts"
https://en.wikipedia.org/wiki/Historical_race_concepts#:
~:text=history%20of%20%22race%22-
,Etymology,1512)%2C%20from%20Italian%20razza.

"How Countries Got Their Names"
https://www.kwintessential.co.uk/blog/translation/count
ries-got-names

"What Every Country's Name Literally Means"
https://www.farandwide.com/s/literal-translations-every-
country-name-a578dd4f1fa7478e

"Were Noah and Abraham Alive at the Same Time"
https://jesusalive.cc/noah-abraham-alive-same-time/

"The History of the Idea of Race"
https://www.britannica.com/topic/race-human/The-
history-of-the-idea-of-race

"What Is A Samaritan?"
https://www.gotquestions.org/what-is-a-Samaritan.html

For free teaching videos that correspond with this book, as well as other books, products, and materials, go to **ferventfire.com.** For events, booking or the latest updates please visit this site often.

To help us change our nation and publish this book abroad, become a part of the "Read and Share partner publishing program" by gifting this book to your family, friends, church, work associates, local officials, and others. This is achieved through purchasing multiple digital or audio books at discounted rates on our website. Simply gather your friends' names and associated email addresses, enter the information, donate towards the publishing and we will do the rest.

To find us in Tulsa, OK

Go to realchurchministries.com

To become a ministry partner

give online or write us at

Fervent Fire Ministries

315 S. Sheridan Road

Tulsa, OK 74112